War On Debt

Breaking the Power of Debt

Financial Freedom Series, Volume I

by

John Avanzini

HIS Publishing Company
Hurst, Texas

War On Debt —
Breaking the Power of Debt —
Financial Freedom Series, Volume I
ISBN: 1-878605-00-3

First edition, 80,000 copies, 1990
Second edition, 30,000 copies, 1990

Unless otherwise indicated, all Scripture quotations are
taken from the *King James Version* of the Bible.
Cover design and illustration by Bob Haddad

Verses marked *TLB* are taken from *The Living Bible*.
Copyright © 1971. Used by permission of Tyndale House
Publishers, Inc., Wheaton, Illinois 60189. All rights
reserved.

HIS Publishing Company
P. O. Box 1096
Hurst, Texas 76053

Contents

This book is dedicated to my son,
David Christian Avanzini,
who faithfully labors
with his mother and me
in the Gospel of Jesus Christ

This publication is part of the three-part Financial Freedom Series consisting of _War On Debt_, _Rapid Debt-Reduction Strategies_, and a debt-reduction workbook. This series is designed to help Christians become debt free by exercising scriptural principles. Its purpose is to give you information and suggestions, not specific directions. Before you make any changes in your current financial structure, it is recommended that you seek counsel from your attorney or accountant.

A Personal Word from the Author

There is a word of financial deliverance in this book for you! It is a word that God wants planted deep within your spirit. You have asked Him for a book like this time and again. Now, **He has placed it in your hand.** On the following pages, the revelation knowledge that you have been seeking concerning your debt problems **is clearly explained.**

Beloved, there is no question about it. The world has come to the end of time. God is revealing to prophets everywhere that He is about to release a **supernatural financial miracle** into His Church. Make no mistake! **It will happen** in these very times in which we live!

Timing is vital to every revelation. If Israel had properly discerned the time of their divine visitation, a Jewish author, instead of John Avanzini, would be writing this book to you.

My prayer for you is that you will rapidly move into the knowledge of this revelation. It is a realm of financial breakthrough that will allow you to function in true biblical prosperity, free from want, and best of all, **free from debt.** From this new position of financial strength, you will be able to give abundantly to the cause of Jesus Christ wherever and whenever you see a valid need.

It is because of faithfulness to God's Word and deep respect for the things that He has shown me from it that I share these truths with you. I believe this book contains vital spiritual revelation concerning your personal finances that **has not previously been heard by our generation.**

I do not make this statement because of some misguided notion of my own brilliance. I say it because of the **brilliance of the Holy Spirit** who has revealed it to me for these last days.

May this timely message from God's Word touch your life at your point of greatest need. May it **root out** the popular philosophy of **deficit-spending,** and permanently release you into the joy of **a debt-free life.**

John Avanzini

1

God's Miraculous Solution to Your Debt Problem

"Is any thing too hard for the Lord?. . ."
Genesis 18:14

A strong sense of hopelessness. . . . That is the way many Christians describe their inner feelings about their finances. They feel as if they are aimlessly adrift in an endless stream of borrowing. Unpaid bills occupy more and more of their thoughts. They honestly believe there is no way out of their debt dilemma.

Please note that I am not speaking of dishonest people, but hard-working, honest folks who are doing all they know to do. However, try as they may, they keep sliding further and further into debt.

The Joy Is Gone

In most homes, both husband and wife are forced to work. Yet, even with two wage-earners, money always seems to be in scarce supply.

For most families, the joy is gone from payday. All that remains is the Friday night ritual of rushing the paycheck to the bank so the checks they wrote Thursday will not bounce. After the paycheck is deposited, they draw out a few dollars from the automatic teller machine for their once-a-week, Friday-night splurge. This consists of a modest meal at a fast-food restaurant and a short walk through the mall. Long gone are the days of shopping, for **they must now pay for their past credit sprees.**

For a pitiful, few hours, the wage-earner feels good, enjoying a small portion of the fruit of his labor. All too soon Saturday morning arrives, and with it comes the full reality of the fruit of debt. The wage-earner must now face his **mountain of bills** — bills that were only partially paid last payday.

God Is Left Holding the Bag

Check after check is written until, finally, the last pressing obligation is paid. With this task accomplished, the stark reality comes to light. There is only enough left to barely scrape by until next payday.

In the crushing pressure of having only enough to make ends meet, **the tithe,** which is so vital to receiving God's blessings in life, is usually ignored. At best only a portion of it is paid. This is usually justified with a promise that soon things will be better, and then God will get what is His.

For the next six days, the average wage-earner has to put off having any fun or doing anything special. To the Christian, the most painful part of this existence is **having to say "No" to God concerning giving into His Kingdom. This is an empty cycle that is routinely made from Friday** to Friday by those who have come under the control of the spirit of debt.

Wake Up to a Better Way!

Wake up! That's no way for the Children of God to live! Surely this is not God's best for your life! He must have a better plan. Deep down in your spirit, you know He wants something more for your life than **barely existing from payday to payday!**

Hear the good news! The same God who wants you to walk in His saving grace, the same God who wants you to experience His miracle healing power, the same God who wants your family to be entirely whole **also wants you to operate in total financial abundance.**

The precious truths you will be studying in this book — the principles of biblical economics — are clearly stated in God's Word! If you follow them, they will free you of your **payday-to-payday blues.** From them you will learn how to boldly get started on your road to a debt-free lifestyle.

A Progressive Walk

God is as concerned about your financial success as He is about every other part of your life.

When you first started to walk with Him, you had to learn to recognize the lies of the devil. They were holding you captive. The world had taught you that drinking and parties were the fun way to live. But as you progressed in your Christian walk, you realized that kind of thinking is flawed. You began to understand that drinking almost always leads to alcoholism, and wild parties open the door to sexual sins. You found that if you were to experience God's best, you would have to say "*No*" to sin, and "*Yes*" to God's way of doing things.

The further you walked in God's ways, the less complicated your world became. Inner peace began to grow. Much to your own surprise, you started having more fun instead of less fun. Since the troubles and torments that accompany the world's wicked ways have begun to melt away, your life has become much more worthwhile.

Well, Child of God, I've got good news for you. This same freedom that you are experiencing in this area of your life is also available to you in your finances!

Please do not misunderstand. **This book has not been written to force you into the lifestyle of a miser.** It is written so that you might experience **a miracle** in your finances—a miracle that will transform your finances from **barely making it** to **abundance**, from **not enough** to **more than enough**, from **little** to **much!**

Recognize the Cause of Your Problem

Before you can participate in this miracle transition, it is important that you recognize some things. **Lies and deceptions** are responsible for your paycheck-to-paycheck existence. Following the world's system of finance instead of God's way is what has brought you to financial shambles. Make no mistake about it. **The world system has enslaved you.**

You must identify the subtle deceptions of this system. You must see how these lies have drawn you into your current financial problems.

The Die Is Cast In Early Childhood

Most Americans bring up their children in homes with **thirty-year mortgages.** They deliver those same precious children to neighborhood schools in the latest, most up-to-date automobiles with **five-year loans.** They buy these children new school clothes with plastic credit cards that charge as high as **twenty-one percent interest** per year! They wash those same clothes in washing machines that have been financed on the department store's **revolving charge account.**

Their children sleep on **mortgaged** *beds.* They sit on **mortgaged** *furniture.* They watch a large-screen, color *television set* which will hopefully be paid off before it falters and breaks down. *Vacations* are routinely paid for with convenient **monthly payments.** The children do their homework using *encyclopedias* and *computers* that are bought on **credit.**

The average Christian child is **born into a family that is in debt.** During his childhood, he **never sees that family come out of debt.** Is it any wonder that after eighteen years of development under this influence, the spirit of debt has been transferred to this impressionable child?

The Ritual of Maturity

Debt has become a ritual of maturity in America. Upon graduation from high school, parents proudly take their child down to the local bank. There they lovingly co-sign a loan for his very first car. With this action, they unwittingly launch him into his own **ocean of red ink.** Parents do this, sincerely believing they have given their child a real "head start" by establishing his credit rating early!

That's crazy! How much of a head start is this innocent child really receiving? He will probably begin his adulthood earning little more than minimum wage, yet he will owe the bank between five and fifteen thousand dollars on, of all things, a rapidly depreciating automobile!

This new debt has not helped him out one bit. Instead, his parents have just given their permission for the bank to hold their precious child in bondage. They have helped him pledge 1,000 to 3,000 hours of his life to serve the lender!

If what I am saying sounds too harsh, just think about it for a few minutes. Remember, any truth that goes against common beliefs is never accepted easily. But please keep your spirit open, and *consider the entire matter before you react*. I am teaching a **tradition-breaking truth!**

This young adult is now deeply indebted to the bank. He has promised to pay them a whopping **twenty-five to seventy-five weeks of his pay.** This represents six months or more of his meager wages. It is an obligation that can take as much as five years of his life to fulfill. If that's not a form a bondage, **what is it?**

A Basic Premise Is Ignored

Now, what makes this premature initiation into debt even more amazing is that it is done without understanding that a basic scriptural premise is being ignored. When we bring up our children in this kind of a debt-laden atmosphere, we overlook one of **God's clear warnings.**

> **"Train up a child in the way he should go: and when he is old, he will not depart from it."**
> **Proverbs 22:6**

But wait, there's more. There is a startling truth that the Church must learn. Scripture taken out of its biblical context usually does not clearly convey the message of God. Instead it conveys the meager thoughts of man. In our everyday interpretation of this verse, the importance of early training is said to be the main lesson. However, if you want some real revelation, look at this often-quoted Scripture in its full context.

> **"Train up a child in the way he should go: and when he is old, he will not depart from it.**

The rich ruleth over the poor, and the borrower is servant to the lender."
Proverbs 22:6,7

Amazing! Train a child to function in debt, and that child will not depart from it when he becomes an adult! How in the debt-ridden world have we overlooked this most obvious scriptural warning? Let that sink into your spirit for a moment; then read verse seven again.

"The rich ruleth over the poor, and the borrower is servant to the lender."
Proverbs 22:7

Do you see what we have been missing? Train up your child to be a debtor, and you have sentenced that child to **a lifetime of servitude to the lender!**

When you consider the clear teaching of these two dynamic verses in their biblical context, you have but one rational choice. **A drastic change** must take place in your thinking and in the thinking of your children. Otherwise, generation after generation will continue to march their unsuspecting children down this deceptive road **into the eager clutches of the spirit of debt.**

A Miracle Is Needed

When I speak of a drastic change, I mean nothing short of a **miracle —a miracle that will rapidly take you out of debt.**

Does such a miracle exist? Can we actually go forward in some financial healing line and walk away with all of our bills marked **paid in full?**

"Why Brother John, if that were so, the person who had that power should immediately bring this miracle to every family in the world. And that's not all he should do! He should then go to every Church that is under the bondage of debt, and set them free."

If this type of logic has a familiar ring, it should! It is the same reasoning used by those who are skeptical of miracle healing. Those same sincere folks say, "If anyone really had the power to heal people, he should go to every hospital and heal everyone."

If there was a man alive today who could miraculously heal people, he would be insensitive if he did not at least heal all the sick folks he met. In the same way, if there was a person who could miraculously release people from the awful burden of their debts, that person would be mean indeed if he did not do so.

Before we go any further, let us get one thing straight. No man has the ability to miraculously heal anyone! **Neither is there anyone who can miraculously release people from their debts!** Beloved, the fallacy of this thinking is that miracles are from **men.** They are not from men. Miracles are given by **God** and received, through faith, by men.

I have laid hands on many people and seen them healed; however, **I have never healed anyone.** Each time someone has been miraculously healed, that person had to receive the miracle from God.

The same biblical principle applies to **the miraculous release from debt.** Each time the miracle of debt cancelation takes place, it comes directly from God to those who receive it through faith.

A Widow Received This Miracle

Make no mistake about it. The miracle of canceled debt is taught in God's Word. One very powerful illustration involves a widow woman and her two sons.

This widow was left with a great debt at her husband's death. She was hopelessly bound until the miracle of debt cancelation set her free. Her debt was so large that her two sons were sentenced to become bond-servants to the creditor. It took everything she had. She was left with nothing more than a small pot of oil. She was brought to the very door of destitution. In her advanced years, she was cruelly sentenced to the life of a beggar.

Thank God for her faith. Her decision not to seek help from the creditor proved to be the wisest move of her life. In the midst of her desperate problem, **she turned to her man of God.** All the creditor could offer her was **more debt,** but God presented her with the opportunity to receive the miracle of canceled debt. All she had to do was exercise the faith to do exactly what her man of God told her to do.

The following verses tell us about her powerful miracle of debt cancelation.

> "Now there cried a certain woman . . . unto Elisha, saying, Thy servant my husband is dead. . . and *the creditor is come* to take unto him my two sons to be bondmen.
> And Elisha said unto her. . . what hast thou in the house? And she said, . . . a pot of oil.
> Then he said, Go, borrow thee vessels. . .
> And when thou art come in, thou shalt. . . pour out into all those vessels, and thou shalt *set aside that which is full* . . . .
> And it came to pass, when the vessels were full . . . the oil stayed.
> Then she came and told the man of God. And he said, *Go, sell the oil, and pay thy debt* . . . ."
> **II Kings 4:1-7**

There it is, right from the pages of your own Bible! A miraculous cancelation of debt! The scriptural account of this particular event opened with an impossible mountain of debt. It demanded payment. Even if it meant the ruination of the woman and her two sons, it had to be paid. Then, in just a few hours, this woman was completely debt free!

With this miracle from God's Word, we see proof positive that He has a miraculous solution for the debt problems of people just like you and me. In the following chapters, you will learn just how badly this miracle is needed.

2

Up to Our Eyeballs In Debt!

"...the borrower is the servant of the lender."
Proverbs 22:7

The amount of money the average family owes to banks, department stores, and other lending institutions has risen every year for the past thirty years. Consumer debt has increased at an even higher rate than the cost of living. It now represents a much larger **percentage** of the average worker's earnings.

Thirty years ago, only about ten percent of individual earnings was being spent on consumer debt. Today, that figure has risen to a staggering nineteen percent. That means almost one-fifth of the average person's earnings is now spent to service his ever-increasing debt!

American consumer debt grew by almost $50 billion in the twelve months of 1988. This brought the total to about $700 billion dollars! This means that if the present debt were to be evenly divided among every man, woman, and child in the United States, they would each owe about $2,800. Now, mind you, that is only consumer debt. This figure does not include the more than $1 trillion (1000 billion) that the American public owes to various lending institutions on their home mortgages.

The Wild Card

Today, plastic credit cards make consumer borrowing easier than ever before. These cards are rapidly adding to the whopping debt that is now taking nineteen percent of all household income.

Credit cards are much easier to abuse than bank loans. The reason for this is that they do not require the borrower to fill out lengthy forms. Neither do they require him to personally sit down with a loan officer and discuss his ability to repay. Instead, many pre-approved credit cards now arrive through the mail. No consultation with the bank is necessary, so the already over-extended borrower can go out that very day and add $500 to $2500 to his debt.

Large-scale distribution of pre-approved credit cards is unique to our generation. Before their advent, American Christians were not nearly as pre-disposed to purchasing consumer goods on credit. Easy access to these plastic charge cards has resulted in the Christian community finding itself in a position of higher debt than ever before. This one strategy of the devil has done more to enslave God's children than any other.

Credit-Card Junkies

Many people in our generation are actually **addicted to credit card debt.** These people have been given their own special name. They are called **"credit-card junkies."** Just like the "junk-food junkies" who cannot control their appetite for unhealthy foods, these financial junkies cannot control their appetite for **compulsive buying.**

This compulsion quickly finds them over their heads in debt. These impulsive spenders do not give a moment's consideration to how their actions will effect their already limited finances. With the mere presentation of their "plastic power," they can plunge themselves and the ones they love yet further into the "bottomless pit of debt."

One recent news story told of a man who owed the unbelievable amount of $67,000 on his multiple credit cards. With this balance, his minimum payment was over $6,200 per month. This amount represented **twice** his entire family's monthly income.

Pre-approved credit cards in the hands of a compulsive shopper can spell the end of that person's happiness. It can cause him to lose **everything he has.**

Plastic Status Symbol

Just as one of the rituals in our society is that first car loan, the credit card has also become **a status symbol of adulthood.** We all probably know a young person, just fresh out of high school, who proudly displays his first credit card. He now has plastic power to add to his status. Everyone is immediately impressed, especially his admiring parents. This seems so mature, until the card is charged to its limit in the first month.

Tiny Tot Credit Cards

A bank in Denver, Colorado, recently announced a plan to issue credit cards to children as young as **twelve years old!** It is hard to believe a society can be this irresponsible and continue to exist. Surely the writer of Proverbs was correct when he said:

> "Train up a child in the way he should go: and when he is old, he will not depart from it.
> The rich ruleth over the poor, and *the borrower is servant to the lender.*"
>
> Proverbs 22:6,7

What more can be said? Credit cards are one of the primary contributors to the debt problems of the American family. If it were only the problem of the non-Christian, it would be terrifying enough. But this same mania is rampant in the Church. Plastic power has quickly driven the average Christian to his knees, not in prayer, but under the load of debt he must now bear.

Skyrocketing Bankruptcies

Naturally, with our nation's steadily increasing credit-card debt, there comes a steadily decreasing ability to pay that debt. Daily television commercials encourage those with financial difficulty to come on down to the attorney's conveniently located offices, and he will make your money problems just go away. All of this will be done by the world's miracle of debt cancelation— **bankruptcy!**

Since 1984, there has been a sharp increase in personal bankruptcies across our nation. This number reached an alarming 550,000 cases in 1988. It is up ninety percent since 1984! That's a ninety percent increase in just six years!

The ease of getting into debt with credit cards, and the willingness of consumers to use them, are the major contributors to this skyrocketing increase. Add the recent liberalization of the federal government's bankruptcy laws, and the removal of the **social stigma** of bankruptcy itself, and you have an **explosive situation.**

The Counterfeit Miracle

Have you noticed there is always a counterfeit to God's miracle? Instant debt cancelation through bankruptcy is no exception. It is an attempt by the devil to counterfeit God's miraculous cancelation of debt; **but do not be deceived.** The world's ways are not God's way.

> "As is the *earthy*, such are they also that are *earthy:* and as is the *heavenly*, such are they also that are *heavenly*."
>
> **I Corinthians 15:48**

Please note, I am not against the bankruptcy laws of our land. They are not wrong when they are applied for their **intended purposes.** There are circumstances in which they are very good. However, they are **immoral** when they become an **easy fix** for irresponsible, reckless spending.

The Banks Own Our Nation's Homes!

The one material thing that Americans have traditionally treasured throughout the decades is **individual home ownership.** But now, the very homes that provide the foundation of the American dream, and in most cases, the primary source of financial security, are being placed in **great jeopardy.**

The American tradition has always been for a young couple to purchase a home so that in their senior years, the home is debt free. This has operated as a form of security for them in their retirement years. But *not anymore.* Instead, when the mortgage is paid down, the banks are now openly encouraging home owners to borrow against their equity. Here is the shocking truth to this deception. **Thirty percent of all home equity loans are used to repay other debts!**

The federal government has actually helped encourage this type of borrowing, for home mortgage interest is one of the few tax deductions remaining for the average American.

Now the purchase of new cars or other "high-ticket" items is being called a tax-smart move when bought through second and third mortgages on the home. This is being recommended by financial planners and many tax experts, because the interest can still be deducted. As a result, home equity (retirement security) has little opportunity to build. The participant remains deep in debt for the entire span of his life. He never builds the much needed retirement nest egg that the debt-free home affords!

Your Hidden Debt

Most people would be shocked if they understood just how great a hold the spirit of debt has on our nation. The average American had to work 124 days in 1989 — a whopping thirty-four percent of the year — just to pay his federal, state, and local taxes!

Talk about being in bondage to the creditor! You have to work **four full months** of every year just to pay your taxes! (Please keep in mind that this does not include even one of your personal debts.)

In 1989, "Tax Freedom Day," the day the average American finally paid off his debt, was May 4. Each year this date is pushed a few days farther into the year. Looking at it on a daily basis, the average worker toiled two hours and forty-three minutes out of every eight-hour day to satisfy his 1989 tax debt! This means that every day, you had to work two hours and forty-three minutes for the government before you began to earn any money for yourself.

In 1981, the American worker paid Social Security taxes at the rate of 6.65 percent of the first $29,700 earned, or a total maximum tax of $1,975. In 1989, the Social Security tax rate rose to 7.51 percent of the first $48,000, which equals an unbelievable maximum tax payment of $3,605. Social Security taxes alone have gone up over eighty-two percent in the past eight years! That is more than a ten percent increase per year!

Your Total Debt Increases Daily

The federal government will collect roughly $1.07 trillion in revenue in 1990. That's up $86 billion from 1989. Surely this is enough! But, no! The Congressional Budget Office still predicts there will be a $155 billion deficit!

In March of 1989 alone, the nation's budget deficit climbed to a staggering $35.78 billion. That's up 22.2 percent from the same month just a year earlier!

Although federal revenues were increased 3.9 percent, government spending shot up 9.5 percent. President Bush's administration estimated the 1989 deficit would total $163.3 billion. That is an increase of 5.3 percent from the $155.1 billion shortfall posted in fiscal 1988.

Here's a number that should stagger your imagination:

$2,775,874,961,565.00

That figure was calculated on April 17, 1989, by the Bureau of Public Debt. It represents the total indebtedness of the government of the United States of America on that day. That is how much money we, the American public, owed, and the amount has steadily grown since then.

On average, the national debt grows at the rate of $722 million per day! This means that by August 17, 1989, the government's debt went up approximately another $87 billion! And it shows no sign of stopping. It just keeps getting worse!

You Pay for the Bankers' Party

On August 9, 1989, President Bush signed into law the biggest taxpayer bailout in history! The cost for the bailout of the savings and loan industry is staggering. Estimates are that it will total over $1,000 for every man, woman and child in the United States before it is complete. The estimated cost is $306 billion. That is bigger than the bailouts of Chrysler Corporation, Lockheed, New York City, and postwar Europe's Marshall Plan combined.

To show you just how blind a nation can become, just hear what else took place. In the same month, congress easily passed a foreign aid package to send $14.3 billion to other nations, including $3 billion for Israel, $2.1 billion for Egypt, and $85 million in military aid to the newly elected government of El Salvador.

Also in that same month, President Bush announced the cancelation of the debt of sub-Saharan African countries to the United States, an amount that is said to be $4.3 billion!

By now, your head is probably dizzy from all these huge numbers, so let me bring it all down to statistics that will make some sense to you. If you had all of your own personal debts paid off, and if you did not owe anybody anything, your personal share of our federal government's debt would still be **$11,209.54**. Remember, this is the amount each man, woman, boy and girl owes. If you are the average American family, you have a spouse and two children. That means your total family debt is $44,838.16! (If you have more than two children, add $11,209.54 for each additional child.)

This debt increases about $3 each day for every man, woman and child. In one year, that amounts to $1,095. This dollar amount represents what the federal government has spent, above the amount they have collected. This is over and above the taxes you have already worked until May 4th to pay!

The World Is Drunk On Debt!

The spirit of debt is not limited to America. Mexico, for example, is currently suffocating under an unmanageable debt load. In 1970, Mexico's foreign debt was less than $5 billion. In just nineteen years, it grew to $100 billion.

In 1989, Mexico had to pay $7 billion in principal payments and an unbelievable $12 billion in interest to its multitude of creditors. Mexico's $19 billion **debt payment** for 1989 was almost four times the amount of their **total debt** in 1970! President Carlos Salinas de Gortari states, "The foreign debt burden has put the brakes on our national progress. It threatens to break up the entire social and economic fiber of the Mexican community. If this excessive transfer of our resources abroad persists, all will be lost."

Third-world developing countries now owe a total debt of $1.3 trillion. In 1987, sub-Saharan Africa alone owed $137.8 billion in medium and long-range debt. The amount of the payment to service these debts rose from $5.6 billion in 1979 to $21 billion in 1989. That is a 400% increase in ten years, or forty percent per year.

The spirit of debt is rapidly spreading across the earth. It is more infectious than any other disease on the planet. During the eighties, Americans, like their government and the governments of other countries, have overdosed on deficit spending and debt. This has brought us to the nineties with nothing more than **promissory notes in the world's coffers.**

Going Under In Good Times

Credit counseling services report a shocking sixty-seven percent increase in the number of clients coming in for help over the past four years. This rapid increase of people owing more money than they can repay would be somewhat understandable if our economy were in a state of depression. But it is not! This increase of financial problems is taking place in the midst of unprecedented financial growth in the American economy!

A Federal Reserve Board economist in Washington, D.C., says historical patterns have gone crazy. It seems contrary to logic that so many Americans would owe so much in a time when financial growth across this nation is rampant.

Tipping Instead of Tithing

The April, 1988, issue of "Christian Retailing" carried an article by Ralph Rath which revealed that the average charismatic Christian spends only $2.17 per week on all Christian-related items. Mind you, that's not just in tithes and offerings. It represents what he spends on **all** Christian causes!

Let this sink in! American Christians spend thirty-four percent of their wages to pay Caesar (the government), while they spend less than two percent on all Christian endeavors combined. This leaves God with nothing more than a tip!

A Prophetic Word

Starting right now, the word from God to His Church is, **"Get out of debt!"** The nineties will be perilous years for planet Earth. The creditor is at the world's door, and **the mortgage is due.** There is nowhere to hide. Pastors used to preach about payday someday. Well, that day has come, and the **cupboard is bare.**

The spirit of debt has driven the world into a most uncomfortable position. **Individuals,** as well as **nations,** find themselves up to their eyeballs in debt. They do not seem to realize that the end of the good life is soon to come, even though every day it becomes more obvious that ever-increasing debt cannot continue.

Worst of all, Christians have blindly followed the lost into this pit. Oh, that they might wake up before **the trap closes behind them!**

Footnote: *All statistics were complied by Christian Services Network, El Cajon, California.*

3

The Trap Closes

"But their minds were blinded. . . ."
II Corinthians 3:14

Victims of seducing spirits follow the path to destruction without reason. The spirit of lust will drive a man and woman to risk family, friends, and social standing for a few moments of carnal satisfaction. There is no logic to this, yet their lustful actions drive them with open eyes to their own ruination.

Likewise, the spirit of greed will drive an already prosperous businessman to become involved in illegal schemes just to secure a few more dollars. He will knowingly risk the loss of his business, and even jail, in his obsession. These illogical, greedy actions usually lead to the loss of all that is important to him.

The same is true with the **spirit of debt**. Just like any other vile spirit, it operates without logic, bringing its victims to destruction without apparent sense or reason. It uncontrollably drives the debtor to deceive himself and his creditors. He is lulled into thinking that his latest whim will bring him the happiness he seeks.

Much of the consumer debt of our nation is totally illogical. It can only be explained as a vile manifestation of **the devil himself.** Satan has found a way to stop the financial prosperity that the Church is beginning to enter in these last days. With the advent of the faith teaching of the last two decades, the Church is learning to walk in the abundance that is needed. But the members are using this abundance for the wrong purpose. Instead of financing the end-time harvest, it is being used for down payments and monthly installments.

The Party Is Over

By some weird stretch of the imagination, borrowing might have made some sense when inflation was running wild during the early seventies. Many economists in those days openly taught that it was wise to purchase tangible items such as a car, a television, or a washing machine on credit, and then pay later with cheaper, inflated dollars.

At that time in history, loans had low, **fixed** interest rates that could not rise with inflation. Along with this, all the interest on those loans was **fully tax deductible**. But that is not the case today. Circumstances have changed! Almost all logical reasoning for buying items on "time" is now becoming extinct. There are three primary reasons for this.

1. Inflation no longer out-strides interest rates. This has lessened the chance of cheaper dollars in the foreseeable future.

2. Interest rates have escalated. Today most lenders charge between eighteen and twenty-one percent interest

to finance household items. The lower interest rates of the seventies seem to be gone forever.

3. Tax deductions are quickly drying up. The once attractive tax incentive for borrowing is going, going, and almost gone.

By the end of 1989, the Internal Revenue Service only allowed a twenty percent write-off of consumer loan costs. In 1990, it has dropped down to only ten percent. In 1991, zero percent. They will allow nothing. **The party will be over.** From that date on, **you are on your own!**

Satan's trap will be sprung. Whoever is caught inside the debt cycle when the trap closes will be eaten alive by the horror of ever-increasing interest due on worn-out products.

Bait and Switch

There is an old trick that con-men use to catch those they would cheat. They call it "bait and switch." This is the way it works. First, an attractive incentive is given. Then, when you take the bait, they switch you to the product they want you to buy — the product that meets **their goals** instead of yours.

This trick has been used on the public. Interest rates are greatly influenced by the government (the world's system), and they are the ones who allow or disallow the tax credits. The **bait** was cheap interest and interest tax deductions.

Now, see the **switch.** Whatever the government gives, **it can take away!** And it has taken away both the cheap interest and the liberal tax deductions. This has left the average American consumer with unmanageable debt.

The elimination of tax-deductible interest on consumer goods will make interest rates of eighteen to twenty-one percent seem much more expensive and devastating to the family budget than ever before!

Lifetime Servants of the Creditor

As convenient as a credit card may seem to be, it is among the most expensive ways ever devised to borrow money. To give you a little idea of just how expensive it is, an eighteen percent annual finance charge will cause your debt to **double** in only four years!

To make sure you are in no hurry to pay off your debt, lenders often make very little demand on the borrower. They only require a very small, minimum payment each month. The minimum is usually around two and a half percent of the entire bill. This low amount is purposely designed so it will be easy, convenient, and painless to pay, or should I say, **not to pay.** This allows your interest cost to skyrocket.

Are the credit card companies interested in whether or not you own the good things in life? Could it be their only concern is that you pay off your bill **as slowly as pos-**

sible, so they will receive the highest possible return on their loan to you?

Here is a shocking statement. You should write it out on a three by five card and put it on top of your stack of bills. You should read it virtually every time you pay them.

If you make the minimum payments on your credit cards and continually use your line of credit to the limit, you will be paying on your cards for the rest of your life. **They will never be paid off.**

Are You In the Trap?

To begin to evaluate the seriousness of your own debt crisis, there are some basic rules established **by the credit industry** to help you know **when you are in trouble.** Naturally, the objective of this book is to help you get entirely out of debt, but as a **first step,** it is important for you to realize how deep into debt's dungeon you have already fallen.

Remember, **the following are not my recommendations or guidelines;** they are the established guidelines of those who openly declare that they want you to be **in debt!**

1. You are in trouble when you pay more than twenty percent of your **gross income** on consumer debt. That includes credit card purchases, personal and student loans — everything but your mortgage. If you are spending more than that, the credit industry says you're stretching yourself too thin.

Since the average American's consumer debt is nineteen percent of his **net income**, we see that most people must be over the limit in this very first test.

2. You are in trouble when you can only afford to pay the minimum monthly payments on your credit-card debt.

Isn't that strange? You are encouraged to pay the minimum payment; then when it becomes impossible to do otherwise, **you are in trouble**. I hope you can see the deceptiveness in this.

3. You are in trouble when you start taking those pre-approved credit cards because you have exhausted the current credit limit on the ones you already have.

Ask yourself this question. How can creditors grant a pre-approved credit card to a person who is already up to his limit in debt? As strange as this behavior seems, it happens every day.

4. You are in trouble when you use credit cards to pay the minimum payment for other credit cards. For example, it is not wise to get a cash advance from one of your bank cards to make payments on your other bills.

I won't even comment on this foolishness!

5. You are in trouble when you make alternating bill payments. You say to yourself, "This month I'll pay my

student loan, next month I'll pay my department store account," and so on.

Please believe me. You are more than just in trouble. When this pattern begins, you are only days from **total financial collapse**.

At one time or another, you might have fallen into one or all of these categories, but don't feel lonely. The spirit of debt is also upon the greater part of your Christian brethren. And no wonder.

It's a Plot

Everything you read in newspapers, magazines, and see on television encourages you to **"go for it."** Buy that expensive new luxury car now! You know it will make you the envy of the neighborhood, and besides that, you will even get $1,000 cash back when you make the purchase.

Take that luxury vacation you so greatly deserve. Fulfill your wildest fantasy. Don't worry about the cost. Take up to sixty months to pay.

Buy the newest line of clothes. In your position, you must make a fashion statement. Wear **now**, and pay **later**!

The size and shape of the various temptations simply does not stop.

Debt is no longer seen as something bad. Instead it is openly encouraged! It has become a **status symbol** and a sign of responsibility. Why, debt has become as American as Mom's apple-pie, baseball, and the flag! Debt has become part of every American's heritage!

We pat each other on the back, wink, and smile as we show off our latest toy — mortgaged, of course. In the midst of all this red ink, we blindly watch our country sink deeper and deeper into irreversible debt. Is there anyone who can deny that the spirit of debt has blinded our spiritual eyes?

> "Having eyes, see ye not? and having ears, hear ye not? ..."
>
> **Mark 8:18**

Only the devil could mastermind such a plot against the inhabitants of planet Earth. It is nothing more than an evil trick to catch the Church and stop Her when God needs Her the most. It is Satan at his worst.

Good Business Practices Are Forced To Go

As strange as it may seem, rampant debt has become a necessity in business. Major corporation managers today are severely penalized for running a debt-free company.

When a public corporation pays off its debt, its stock equity value automatically goes up. This should be good for the business and its stockholders, but it is not. When debt drops, that corporation becomes a prime target for what are called "corporate raiders." These Jesse James's of the twentieth century are able to manipulate the takeover of the company with what are called "junk bonds" (bonds that stand a good chance of never being paid off). As soon as they take over a good, solvent company, they start selling off and mortgaging its assets, making windfall profits from the good management of their predecessors.

In today's corporate world, an executive who faithfully manages the company business affairs is called a **bad manager**, for his actions make the corporation too valuable. Thus, it becomes a **target for takeovers.**

Corporate managers who borrow to the hilt, keeping their corporation at the brink of bankruptcy, are considered **good** managers. As a result, giant interest costs are incurred. The final product of this illogic is that the consumer must pay more at the check-out line.

The Bible warns of a day like this:

> **"Woe unto them that call evil good, and good evil; that put darkness for light, and light for darkness; that put bitter for sweet, and sweet for bitter!"**
> **Isaiah 5:20**

Retiring In an Ocean of Red Ink

Today, more and more of our senior citizens are entering their retirement years strapped with unmanageable debt. This ocean of red ink forces them to sell their homes. This uproots them from their lifetime friends and family, forcing them to move to cheaper locations, even into the dangerous environment of the ghetto.

All of this must be done just to make it possible for them to bear their staggering debt load.

The hope for senior citizens somehow escaping the grip of debt has become even bleaker of late. In the last few years **a horrible new plan** has been developed to capture the last bit of money from the older generation. It is called the reverse mortgage and is only available to those over sixty-two who have debt-free homes.

Here's the way this satanic plan works. The bank will pay up to $1,000 a month to senior homeowners who have already paid off their original mortgages. The lending period lasts until the homeowners sell the house or die. Meanwhile, the bank silently, but surely, receives an ever-increasing percentage of the precious couple's home.

There are nearly nineteen million elderly households in the country. Eighty-three percent of them own their homes, and seventy-three percent own their homes free and clear. Of these, 1.7 million own houses worth more than $50,000 and have an annual income below $10,000. These senior citizens are house-rich and cash-poor.

The reverse mortgage plan sounds like a nice way for them to be able to live in their homes until death. However, it is anything but that. It is actually a deceptive way to rob these folks of their largest tangible asset and leaves them with **nothing to pass on to their children**.

Now, I know we live in an age with bumper stickers on the back of large motor homes that read, "I Am Spending My Children's Inheritance," but beloved, be assured that this is not a biblical quotation. It is exactly the opposite.

Here's what the Bible says about your responsibility to leave an inheritance:

> **"A good man leaveth an inheritance to his children's children. . . ."**
> **Proverbs 13:22**

There it is in black and white. Scripture places a high degree of responsibility on you to provide an inheritance for your children's children (grandchildren)! That's a far cry from the attitude of the Church of our day!

The key that will make it possible for you to leave a proper inheritance for your children and grandchildren is for you to **get out of debt, and stay out of debt!**

If you do this, when you reach retirement age, your **home** will belong to you, not the bank. Your **car** will be yours, not the bank's. Then you will have a **savings account,** and **the bank will owe you money** in the form of interest, instead of your owing the bank.

Rampant debt has become like an infectious disease that weakens every aspect of our society. Not only is it a national disgrace, but it has placed the whole world in jeopardy. As you move into the following chapter, you will clearly see the weight debt places on your shoulders.

Remember! "He that goes borrowing, goes sorrowing."

4

Debt — A Very Heavy Responsibility!

". . . Alas, master! for it was borrowed."
II Kings 6:5

The story I'm about to relate to you is true. It comes from the Bible. It is so simple in its truth that most miss its intended meaning. **Debt brings a staggering burden of responsibility upon the borrower.**

In the previous chapters we saw how debt can force senior citizens to sell their homes and move to remote locations without family and friends. We saw how individuals, and even entire countries, suffocate under the burden of debt. Let us now focus on the staggering consequence of debt as it is shown in the Word of God.

The Prophet's Attention Is Captured

The sons of the prophets were in the process of cutting wood for a new dwelling. To obtain the best beams, they went down to the water's edge where the trees grew tall and straight. As one of them was cutting down a tree, the ax head came loose and fell into the water, promptly sinking to the muddy bottom.

At that very moment, the man of God walked by. The young prophet knew he had but a brief moment to draw the prophet's attention to his desperate problem.

You may wonder why the loss of such a simple thing as an ax head would be called a desperate problem. It seems all that was needed was a voucher for the young man to be reimbursed. With the money, he could buy a new ax head, and all would be well.

Before the true depth of this young man's problem can be understood, there is something you must take into account. The Scripture says this was a very special ax head, for it was borrowed. When an ax head is borrowed, nothing but the safe return of the same ax head, in the same or better condition is acceptable.

Fortunately, this young man understood Elisha's heart. He knew the man of God did not want his people to be in debt to anyone. Because of his insight, he did not simply call out, "Sir, I've lost my ax head." Nor did he say that a very good ax head had fallen into the water. He did not cry out to the prophet that the ax head had great sentimental value, or that it had been in the family for years. Any one of these pleas would probably have brought forth no more than a word of sympathy.

Instead, this young fellow guaranteed the involvement of the man of God in retrieving the ax head by crying out that it was **borrowed!**

> "... and he cried, and said, Alas, master! for it was borrowed."
>
> **II Kings 6:5**

Most people do not understand that when they take responsibility for something that is not their own, their entire emotional being will be shaken if it cannot be returned. When the young man realized he could not repay that which he had borrowed, his responsibility for the ax head immediately began to weigh heavily upon him.

Because It Was Borrowed

How did the man of God respond when he heard that the ax head at the bottom of the river had been borrowed? He immediately realized that this matter went far beyond the mere loss of an ax head. Something had to be done. Everything else had to wait, for the young prophet had allowed himself to become the servant of man (the lender).

> "... the borrower is servant to the lender."
> **Proverbs 22:7**

Nothing short of a miracle could have solved this problem. The young prophet's moment of reckoning was fast approaching. The ax head would soon have to be returned. If it could not be, the testimony of that young man would be tarnished in the eyes of the lender.

Hear the sacred Word as it reveals the prophet's attitude toward the young man's problem.

"And the man of God said, Where fell it? And he shewed him the place. And he cut down a stick, and cast it in thither; and the iron did swim.

Therefore said he, Take it up to thee. And he put out his hand, and took it."

II Kings 6:6, 7

One of the most extraordinary miracles ever performed took place. There was no other reason great enough to merit a **swimming ax head** than the fact that it was borrowed. This immediately changed the importance of this occasion from a **minor** event to a **major** event.

Often this passage is used to illustrate the power of God. Why, He can even make an iron ax head swim! But beloved, that is not the main point being made here. The most important lesson is that **God is concerned about your debt problems!**

Debt Brings Anxiety

Experts tell us that today, as never before, our society is overwhelmed with anxiety. The greatest single reason for this emotional upheaval is attributable to **money problems**. The staggering debt with which most people are forced to live is more than their emotional systems were created to bear.

Please note that I am not speaking of "financial deadbeats" (those who borrow with no intention of repaying). I am speaking of good, honest people who have foolishly acquired more debt than they can repay. Our society is full of these folks. They suffer tremendous psychological pain. Their inability to manage their debts gives them a feeling of hopelessness.

More sleepless nights are attributed to unmanageable debt than to anything else. This has been greatly responsible for America becoming an around-the-clock society. Stores, television stations, and bars remain open twenty-four hours a day, primarily catering to the needs of the sleepless.

A Damaged Fender Can Damage Your Soul

Let me illustrate how devastating the responsibility of debt can be. Have you ever had a little fender-bender with your automobile? When this happens it is traumatic, to say the least. No matter how unpleasant it may be, it is not to be compared to the trauma that the same fender-bender would cause if the circumstances were just a little different. Imagine that you had this same accident in a **borrowed car.** Upon impact, your inner man (soul) would immediately cry out, **"Alas, it was borrowed!"**

No matter how you try, it is next to impossible to completely remedy the damage that is done to something borrowed. It will never be the same again. You can even go out and buy a more expensive model to replace it, but from deep down in your soul, "the accuser" will tell you of your **irresponsibility.** Even if the lender totally forgives you, your soul may be permanently scarred. The impact of not being able to return that which you borrowed in its original condition will leave its mark. Each time you see the one who loaned you the car, you will feel the pain. Personally,

I would rather have my own automobile totally destroyed than to put even a scratch on a borrowed car!

When responsible people borrow, their emotions are always impacted. There is no better way to put it. **Borrowing grinds at your insides.**

Debt Attributes to Divorce

Many Christians have a hard time believing that God is concerned about their finances. Yet all Christians would agree that God has extreme concern for the sanctity of marriage. Well, beloved, here's a simple fact. Unmanageable debt is the leading cause of broken marriages! In 1988 over fifty percent of the 1.3 million newly divorced couples listed **money** (or more precisely, more debt than there was money to repay) as **the main reason** for their divorces.

It's no wonder that financial trouble is the leading cause of divorce. When debt is out of control, wives become **afraid** to answer the telephone. They fear hearing the harsh voice of another bill collector demanding payment. They are **afraid** to answer the door because they may be greeted by one of the utility companies that has come to shut off their service. Every time a truck pulls up on their street, they **fear** it is the man from the finance company coming to take back the television or the family car.

With a day of **debt-induced terror** behind her, you can easily imagine the "warm" greeting this housewife is going to give her already stressed-out husband when he walks in the door. Can you imagine the inadequate feelings this husband experiences as he listens to his wife's broken-hearted description of her day? Do you see how debt tears at marriage?

Christian marriages are not exempt! Husbands become threatened, even intimidated, when they fail to provide the basic necessities for their families. This strikes at the very essence of the husband's manhood.

Breadwinners Become Bread Losers

Even though many wives work outside the home, the husband is traditionally looked upon as the family's **bread-winner**. However, if he fails to adequately provide bread for the family, at least in his own mind, he becomes the family's **bread loser**. Financial failure causes him embarrassment, making him feel unattractive, even unworthy of his wife's attention. When the husband begins to feel inadequate in providing the basic necessities for his family, that family is well on its way to destruction.

The results are predictable. The most intimate relationships in that marriage start to fall apart. All meaningful communication stops as the relentless **pressure** of unpaid bills increases. Loving care is quickly replaced by **short tempers**. Family fights start over such things as whether it is **really** necessary to take junior to the doctor. The real issue ceases to be whether the child needs medical attention, but the underlying issue is **"How in the world will we be able to pay another doctor bill?"**

Divided Families

This same tragic pattern often repeats itself among other family members. When son borrows from father, or when sister borrows from brother, and fails to pay back the debt, something much more serious than the loss of money takes place. Fathers and sons stop talking. Brothers and sisters cease to visit each other. In short, borrowing from relatives often results in a permanent breach in normal family relations.

Broken Friendships

Bad debts quickly break up **lifelong friendships**. When you borrow money from a friend, then cannot pay it back, what happens? Invariably, the friendship begins to weaken, then it just dies. If the amount of the debt was high enough, lifetime friends are turned into **lifetime enemies**.

Good Employees Become Bad Employees

Alcoholism and drug abuse are often triggered by the pressures of unmanageable debt. Previously good employees are driven to poor work habits, crime, or even suicide over their debt problems. Sleepless nights and meaningless days are the result of not being able to pay the bills. Eventually, a good employee becomes a bad one. Letters of commendation turn into **warning notices**, and eventually, the dreaded **pink slip appears**.

The Great Commission Becomes the Great Omission

The over-extended Christian can have little, if any part in the Gospel outreach. Instead of his primary purpose being to reach the world for Christ, he must now allocate all his money to debt payments. To put it simply, **his debt now rules him**. He can no longer properly give to the cause of Christ. His new master will not let him. Debt always says, **"NO!"** to the preaching of the Gospel. For all intents and purposes, the overburdened child of God has, by his own hand, canceled his part in the "Great Commission."

When the spirit of debt rules, the biggest goal the local church has is making the monthly mortgage payment. Satisfying the lender has replaced satisfying God. When this happens, the Church is no longer the servant of God. Her own foolish actions have made her the servant of the lender.

Child of God, I hope the seriousness of this nightmare is beginning to sink into your spirit. **Debt rules! Debt ruins!**

Remember, the Word of God says,

"... the borrower is servant to the lender."
Proverbs 22:7

Forced Bankruptcy Awaits

When you come into uncontrollable debt, no financial decision can be made without first consulting your new ruler, the lender. You cannot go on vacation. You cannot buy desperately needed groceries for the hungry. You cannot even give to the Gospel.

Even if the spirit of God moves you, the lender has the right to say, "**No, I must be paid first!** Until I am paid in full, you are **my** servant, not the Lord's!"

When debt rules, it can even decide that your tithe will not be paid! The courts of the land say so. There is a little-known law in the federal bankruptcy statutes that outlines a simple procedure that can be used by anyone to whom you owe money. This provision of the law allows the lender to tell you how you must spend your money.

If any of your creditors feel they are not being fairly paid out of your income, they can have the bankruptcy court intervene in your financial matters. The court can then tell you whom you can and cannot pay. This procedure is called "involuntary bankruptcy," or creditor-induced bankruptcy. When this happens, the government (Caesar), not God, rules over your finances. You will not be allowed to pay any tithe or offering until every cent is paid to the lenders!

The children of God must understand that when something has been borrowed, the fatal day of reckoning always comes. When it does, nothing short of **payment in**

full will satisfy the lender. God knew precisely what He was saying when He declared:

> **"...the borrower is servant to the lender."**
> **Proverbs 22:7**

Debt is surely an extremely severe form of servitude! It is no wonder that a loving God cares so much about people who are in debt — **people like you!** He does not want His children burdened with this heavy responsibility.

Here is a comforting statement for those of you who still cannot believe that God really cares about such basic things as the bills you owe.

> **"Casting *all* your care upon him; for *he careth for you.*"**
> **I Peter 5:7**

God wants to take the excessive responsibility of the debtor off your back, "for He careth for you!"

5

The Spirit of Debt

". . . we are not ignorant of his devices."
II Corinthians 2:11

By now I hope you realize there is a spirit that pushes people into uncontrollable debt. When I speak of uncontrollable debt, I'm talking about the kind of debt that can no longer be properly serviced by the borrower. I am speaking of people who are **driven** by the **impulse** to buy — an impulse to charge ever more to their already over-extended credit lines. I am talking about folks who will lie to get more credit while they cannot pay off what they already owe.

Impulsive Buyers Are Exploited People

The addiction to credit buying is carefully exploited by many of today's unscrupulous store owners. They strategically place eye-catching "impulse items" at each check-out counter. This selling method is so powerful that mothers have officially complained and headed campaigns against putting such items as candy bars and gum at eye level for their children to see. They claim it causes problems because their little darlings cry incessantly at the market check-out, pleading "Mommy, mommy, please. I want it." As a result of their petitions, some supermarkets now **reluctantly** provide a special check-out counter where these impulse items are not so prominently displayed.

This type of marketing is motivated by the devil's knowledge of the Scriptures. He knows that if you bring up a child to **buy on impulse**, one day that child will be a prime candidate to become the **lender's** servant instead of the **Lord's** servant.

Please make no mistake about it. This compulsion to buy is even stronger among adults than it is among children. Exploitation of the adult consumer is fully exercised.

An Evil, Underlying Plan

Past advertising trends have conditioned the consumer to buy simply because he **"deserves"** it. One very popular fast-food chain further exploits this thinking by saying, **"You deserve a break today."** A manufacturer of an expensive hair-coloring formula says you must buy their over-priced product because **you are "worth it."**

When impulse buying only involves a pack of gum, a candy bar, or a hamburger, it seems innocent enough. But it becomes serious business when it progresses on to high-priced items such as **cars, speedboats, a new home** — items that quickly prove to be too expensive for your already overtaxed budget.

When this compulsion becomes fully developed, the consumer is **driven** to buy, even if he has to charge the item he wants. He begins to shop just to **cheer himself up**. He buys to **reward himself**. He splurges to enhance his feelings of **prestige**. Some call it "keeping up with the Joneses." (By the way, I heard that the Joneses are filing for bankruptcy next week, just ahead of all those who have tried to keep up with them!)

California Recognizes the Spirit of Debt

The spirit that drives people to impulse buying has become so severe that the legislature of California has passed a law that gives people a three-day grace period to return things they buy on a purchase contract (time payments). This statute allows them to return purchases with **no questions asked**. They are released from any financial commitment they may have made to the seller.

Why was this law enacted? Because the California legislature felt it had a responsibility to protect the millions of **impulse consumers** our credit society has produced. Protect them from what, you ask? Protect them from the well-honed practices employed by high pressure salespeople who thrive on the credit addiction of the masses.

Are you understanding what you are reading? The spirit of debt has so weakened the average American's sales resistance that state governments now feel it necessary to enact laws to protect their citizens from it.

A Debt Card, Not a Credit Card

In this debt-crazed society, the spirit of debt drives consumers to **buy on credit**. Actually, that statement is not precisely true. Let me clarify it.

Time-payment buying is not buying on credit, it is buying on debt! That is another statement you should write down on a three by five card and read every day. That knowledge can change your life. Consumers are actually **driven** to buy on **debt**.

Perhaps the most deceptive trick ever pulled by the **spirit of debt** came through the public relations firm that came up with the term "credit card." It sounds good, but the term "credit" is totally misused when it refers to those plastic cards. People who buy with plastic bank cards do not **draw** on their **tangible assets**. They simply **add** to their **tangible debt**. Their bank cards are nothing more than the clever devices of the lender that put the general public ever deeper into debt.

Think about it for a minute. When an accountant does a profile of your financial condition, he puts all your assets in the credit column, and all your debts in the debit column. The credit column reflects those things that are **owned**. The debit column reflects those things that are **owed**.

The full value of your house goes in the credit column. The full value of your new car goes in the same column.

The amount of cash you have on hand in the bank goes there also.

Your credit cards **never** go in the credit column. You own nothing when you own a credit card **except** the right to **immediately** reduce your assets.

You may have a plastic card that says you have $5,000 worth of credit, but **what** does that really mean? Well, we know for sure it doesn't mean you have over-paid the bank, thereby creating a credit of $5,000. All it means is that you have the right to go out and **expand your debt** by $5,000. The term "credit card" is a very subtle and clever marketing ploy to make you feel that you have something **you really don't have**.

If you choose to use your credit card, you can only do one thing with it — **rack up additional debt**. It really ought to be called a **debt card**. It not only allows you to go into more debt, it also allows you to go into the **most expensive type of debt available**. With many of these cards, you will pay the highest interest rate allowed by law.

Credit cards are beginning to be treated in a new way. Most banks now insist that you list your **unused card limits** on your financial statement as well as the balances you owe. They know the average consumer will charge every card right up to the limit in a relatively short period of time.

Is It Possible Banks Want You In Debt?

Whatever you call them — credit cards, plastic bank cards, or debt cards — they can quickly make financial circumstances miserable for a very long period of time. If the greatest of care is not exercised, they will inevitably put the family in financial bondage. And, make no mistake about it. **It appears that is exactly what the lenders want!**

Our society has now evolved to the so-called "civilized" position of not even allowing you to cash your check at the supermarket or department store without a **major** credit card. (Perhaps they are called "major" because they have the potential of getting you into **major** trouble.)

Think about this unusual requirement. Your driver's license is all the police department requires to identify you. If the federal government wants proof positive as to who you are, they will never ask you for a major credit card as proper identification. They will accept your driver's license or social security card, or at the most, your birth certificate, but **never a major credit card**.

Why do retail stores have this strange requirement? The origin of this **unnecessary** piece of identification is easy to determine. It is nothing more than an extension of the deceptive scheme the devil uses to **promote nationwide use of credit cards!** Did the promoters of credit cards get together and come up with this **clever plan** that literally forces every adult American to own at least one major "debt" card?

The Spirit of Debt Is Transferrable

Child of God, use your God-given unction. Aren't you beginning to see that the spirit of debt is **satanic**? It is sent from hell to trap its victims in an ever-increasing pit. How many friends have you heard say, "Oh, I only got a credit card **so I could cash my checks?**" Notice how long it is before they go out and charge its entire $5,000 credit limit on stuff they were living without before they got it. Don't think for a moment that a real, demon spirit cannot be **transferred** into your life through a plastic card.

I was told by one lady that she had such difficulty controlling the use of her debt cards, she froze them in a pan of water. Then, whenever she had the driving urge to use them, she would have to go to the deep freeze with an ice pick and chip away at that block of ice until the cards were free. In the frenzy of chopping through the rock-hard ice, she said she was **usually** able to overcome her impulse to go out and charge.

Don't tell me the spirit of debt cannot be transferred from a plastic card to an unsuspecting child of God! That would be like saying the spirit of alcoholism cannot be transferred through the use of the chemical compound known as alcohol.

Credit Anonymous

If there was no spirit of debt, there would be no need for organizations called "Credit Anonymous." These organizations really exist. They are found in most large cities. They deal exclusively with helping folks who have acknowledged their addiction to plastic bank cards and credit purchasing.

It is not at all surprising that, as a nation, we have become addicted to credit. Before most couples even go to the church to get married, they are already in debt to the bank for new car loans and probably both owe large sums of money for the wedding rings they will "give" each other. With this initiation into the world of debt, it is only a short time before they overdose and become **hopelessly hooked** by the spirit of debt.

Debt Addiction, a Form of Insanity

How many otherwise rational and honest Christians have intentionally falsified loan applications to be able to borrow more money? How many have documented their false claims of high income with copies of altered tax returns to justify a higher loan? Too late, these driven people realized they actually needed the mythical income they claimed to have in order to pay the monthly payments of their increased debt. However, since they did not really earn as much as they claimed, their problem increased.

The only explanation I can find for this type of activity is **temporary insanity.** Can't you hear these folks as they realize what they have done and cry, **"How could we have done such a stupid thing? We must have been out of our minds!"**

A Self-Imposed Sentence on Your Remaining Days

When you buy something on time payments, what you actually do is impose a time sentence upon your life. For example, if a person is thirty years old, and plans to retire at sixty-five, he has thirty-five years of life remaining **to produce income.**

When he secures a thirty-year mortgage for a new home, he is actually passing a thirty-year time sentence on his remaining productive years. That is equivalent to eighty-six percent of his productive financial life. With the single commitment to a thirty-year home loan, he guarantees that the majority of his financial life will be spent in debt to the mortgage holder. His own hand has set him in bondage to the banks for all but five of his financially productive years.

Next, this same person secures a five-year car loan. This single act dedicates fourteen percent of his financial life to paying for that car. When the children reach school age, he takes out a four-year loan to buy encyclopedias. This represents an eleven percent sentence of his financial life.

Do you see how the spirit of debt dominates your wage-earning life?

Your Money Is Your Life

The real issue here is that it takes **time** to earn money, **and time is your very life.** That is why God gave me the statement, *"Your Money Is Your Life."*

Unlike time, money never really gets spent. You can give $20.00 to the grocery store, but it is not spent. It is not gone. It has not become useless. It has only changed hands. The only thing that has really been spent is the **time** it took you to earn the $20.00. Money is always constant. People **spend** their lives to obtain it.

Think of your remaining years as units of life from which you must produce income. That thirty-five years of income-producing time is equal to 1,820 weeks. If you spend a large portion of those weeks on house payments, you have greatly restricted your discretion over those years.

For instance, if the house payment amounts to two weeks of your pay per month, you will spend 720 of your working weeks paying your thirty-year mortgage. If you compare that 720-week loss to your total 1,820 weeks of income-producing time, you will find that only 1,100 working weeks remain uncommitted. A thirty-year mortgage is actually forty-six percent of your remaining income-producing life.

Before you just sign up for thirty years of payments, keep in mind that those thirty-five income-producing years are your most profitable years. They are the ones that give you an opportunity to get ahead in the financial game. They are the years when you should save something for the **future** instead of paying for the **past**.

Credit Report or Tithing Report?

The spirit of debt causes people to give so much attention to their credit records that these become **more important** to them than their tithing records. Malachi 3:8 asks this sobering question:

> "Will a man rob God? Yet ye have robbed me. But ye say, Wherein have we robbed thee? In tithes and offerings."

When we fail to tithe, we actually rob God! No faithful Christian would ever consider stealing from anyone. Christians pride themselves on being honest. Yet many of these same people make a pre-meditated criminal decision to steal from their God every Sunday.

Child of God, whether or not you should tithe is not a decision God has left up to you. It is one of those decisions He has made for you.

> "Bring ye all the tithes into the storehouse...."
> **Malachi 3:10**

> "... all the tithe of the land, whether of the seed of the land, or of the fruit of the tree, is the Lord's: it is holy unto the Lord."
> **Leviticus 27:30**

According to the Word of God, tithing on your increase is **mandatory**. God expects every Christian to be faithful in this matter. It becomes very clear that the spirit of debt has a firm hold on the Church when a tithing report **falls far behind** a credit report **in importance.**

Borrowing To Improve Your Ability To Borrow

To further show you how the spirit of debt rules, consider how many people you know who have actually borrowed money they did not need so they could improve their credit ratings. Most people do this from time to time to increase the amount of money the banks will lend them. Why, you may have done it yourself. But can you imagine these same people going out and borrowing money, and giving it to the church so they can improve their giving records?

Most people have subconsciously removed God from being their source. They have replaced Him with their local lending institutions. God's Word says that He desires to be our source. Even in times of need, He promises to stand by those who properly give to Him.

> "Offer unto God thanksgiving; and pay thy vows unto the most High:
> And call upon me in the day of trouble: I will deliver thee...."
>
> **Psalm 50:14, 15**

I challenge you to find such a guarantee from your bank or lending institution. No matter how faithful you are to your bank, they may not help you when you ask.

Surely the Church made a poor trade when they turned from the living God to the failing banking industry as their source.

Debt Has Become a Sunday-Go-To-Meeting Spirit

Even our churches borrow with little or no thought of what the Bible says about becoming the servant of the lender. The devil is enjoying a definite social advantage, for the spirit of debt is no longer perceived as undesirable by our society.

Unlike the spirit of alcoholism or drug addiction, the spirit of debt is readily acceptable in the Christian community. Yet, the devastation it brings upon our churches easily outweighs the damage caused by drugs and alcohol.

If you doubt that statement, remember that over fifty percent of all failed marriages attribute their divorces to overwhelming debt.

Yes, drugs and alcohol destroy homes, but it is the addiction to debt that sends most couples to the divorce courts.

Not too long ago, a leading talk-show host said, "I have to be wealthy to owe three million dollars." Everyone laughed and snickered. He is typical of the national spirit and attitude that says **debt is okay,** and the more you owe, **the better off you must be!**

Beloved, make no mistake about it, **debt is a spirit.** It has brought the Church **into the world** and the world **into the Church.**

> "... the spirit that now worketh in the children of disobedience."
>
> **Ephesians 2:2**

The spirit of debt has **crossed the line.** It not only works in the children of **disobedience,** but it has been welcomed into the Church and now also works in the children of **obedience.**

The effect of this sanction goes far beyond global implications. The spirit of debt within the Church has definite **eternal** implications! I am convinced that the entire world could be evangelized on the annual interest payment Christians are making to their new master, the lender.

Oh, when will we rid ourselves of the spirit of debt? When will we again give the Great Commission of our Lord its proper priority? When will we again extend our maximum effort to reach the world for Christ? When will we stop following the commission of the devil that encourages us to **"keep up with the Joneses"?** When will we be satisfied to **"keep up with Jesus"?**

I pray for the day when God's children will be able to spend their time **budgeting their giving** instead of scrimping to **budget their living.**

Praise God! This is not a book of problems, it is a book of **solutions!** God has the answer in His sacred Word to break the spirit of debt from your life. His answer is **a miracle.**

Before that miraculous debt cancelation process can be unleashed in your life, you must first become convinced that God's way is the **only real way out** of your financial problem.

> "... call upon me in the day of trouble: I will deliver thee...."
>
> **Psalm 50:15**

For some reason, people do not tend to use God's solution until they know from experience that man's solution does not work. The next chapter will take you one step closer to your miracle debt release by showing you yet another manmade solution **that does not work, "debt consolidation."**

Footnote: See Rapid Debt-Reduction Strategies, Financial Freedom Series, Volume II, for information on how to shorten the length of a mortgage.

6

You Cannot Borrow Your Way Out of Debt

"Hear. . . this, O foolish people. . . without understanding; which have eyes, and see not; which have ears,
and hear not."
                                        Jeremiah 5:21

What a marvelous-sounding concept debt consolidation is! But borrowing your way out of debt is no more
than just another trick to draw you deeper into debt.

Extending, Not Solving the Problem

If too much of your money is going toward your bills,
the world system says, "No problem! Go on down to your
friendly loan officer. He will be glad to consolidate your
many small bills into one giant new bill with a somewhat
smaller monthly payment. Everything will be okay."

There you have it in a nutshell — the creditor's
miracle solution for your financial problems. Just sign the
new loan papers, and you will be free.

Child of God, that's a lie straight from the pit of hell.
What you are hearing is not a new wonder cure for your
debt. It is just one more deception the spirit of debt has

to offer. With your new consolidation loan will also come the fresh temptation to take on some brand new bills.

Hear the spirit of debt as it moves to gobble up the few dollars that consolidation has released. "Why, that new automobile you couldn't possibly afford before can now be yours. Those new clothes that will make you look great for Easter are once again within your grasp. Just sign a six-month note for a few dollars a month, and presto! You are back in style. A vacation is surely in store. It makes sense to rest up a bit before you start paying off the new consolidation loan. *Surely you will now have enough surplus funds to make these few new payments.*"

Step by step, the spirit of debt will draw you even deeper into debt than you were before. Just a few impulsive moves and your bills will once again be out of control. Soon you will owe twice as much as you did before you got involved with the counterfeit miracle called "debt consolidation."

Hear the Truth

Please hear the truth of this matter! **You cannot borrow your way out of debt!**

What a simple statement that is, but how few people actually believe it. You must let it sink deep into your spirit. If this book is to lead you **out of debt**, you must first stop your journey **into debt**. Make no mistake about it. Debt consolidation is nothing more than a fancy word for increasing the amount of money you owe. I say it again. **You cannot borrow your way out of debt!**

A consolidation loan will rarely reduce the total amount of money you owe. Keep this in mind. There will be new loan costs to add to your balance. Your interest costs will also go up because you will be taking much longer to pay off the new loan. Consolidation borrowing almost always **adds** to the total debt.

Think back with me to the last chapter. In it, we referred to debt payments in terms of their being "spent segments" of your life. Each additional year of payment you agree to make with your new consolidation loan represents an extra year of sentence to which you have committed your already limited income-producing life.

Figures Don't Lie

Let us say that your current bills total $10,000, and it will take five years to pay off a consolidation loan at a payment of $265.00 per month. With this loan structure, your new debt, with interest, equals $15,900. If you earn $10 an hour, that means you are sentencing yourself to 1,590 hours of **your life** to work for the lender to pay off the total obligation.

Even with what I have said to this point, the innocent-sounding act of consolidating your debts may still seem like a sensible solution. But let's examine more closely what this fancy-sounding thing called "debt consolidation" really means.

The act of debt consolidation usually results in a somewhat lower monthly payment, but this payment must be made for a much longer period of time. For example, you could also consolidate that same $10,000 debt so that your payments would drop to half the $265 we used in the first illustration. This would make your new payment only $132.50 per month.

Great! It sounds as if you just saved $132.50 each month! Not so. The term of the lower monthly payment will now be twelve years instead of five years. So, your true total debt will go up to $19,080, and the **time** it will take you at $10 an hour to pay off that new, easy-payment consolidation loan is 1,908 hours.

In the process of this new debt consolidation, you have **increased the sentence you must serve to pay off that debt by 318 precious hours of your income-producing life!**

You see, it is a true statement. **You cannot borrow your way out of debt!** You can only borrow your way **deeper into debt**.

A Few Rare Instances

The only way debt consolidation can help you out of debt is if you can get the interest on your total bills reduced. This will cause the debt to be paid off more quickly because more of each payment will be going toward paying off the balance of your loan. Usually the only circumstance in which this can happen is when you owe large amounts of high-interest credit card debts. They can sometimes be consolidated into a second mortgage on your home which often bears a lower interest rate. This type of loan can also have an additional advantage. It may be tax deductible.

Consolidation by a finance company or bank usually will not reduce your total cost in terms of time served to pay off your debt. These institutions almost always charge a higher interest rate because they recognize that you are a poor money manager. Your risk of default or bankruptcy has increased since you made the original bills.

"Debt consolidation", like "credit card," is simply another nice-sounding public relations term that money lenders use to capture more and more of your income-producing life. It is for the benefit of the lender, not the borrower. Consolidation is done for three basic reasons:

1. It discourages bankruptcies.
2. It gives the lender a chance to adjust the interest rate upward.
3. The lender has the opportunity to add collateral to the loan.

Remember, the true cost of any debt is the **time** you must work to pay off the loan. Extending the length of time it takes you to pay off your bills is not God's best for you!

God's Ways Are Better Ways

Scripture surely offers a better answer to your debt problem than loan consolidation. God's solution is always better than the world's solution.

When God saved you, He did not just temporarily cover your sins. He permanently washed them away by the blood of Jesus Christ. In the process of divine healing, God does not temporarily remove sickness from you. When he heals, it is total healing.

The same pattern of deliverance also applies to your financial problems. Yes, God has provided a way to get you **totally** out of debt. He has something much better in mind than an extension of what you owe.

I do hope that by now these words have stopped sounding strange to you. In the next few chapters you are going to read more about the **divine miracle of canceled debt.** It appears throughout the Word of God.

Please believe me, while this might sound too good to be true to the debt-ridden of our society, this concept is by no means foreign to the Bible. The Scriptures speak **clearly** and **frequently** about the miracle of canceled debt. If it still seems impossible, ask yourself this question:

"Is any thing too hard for the Lord? . . ."
Genesis 18:14

The answer is, No!

7

The Miracle of Canceled Debt

"All scripture is given by inspiration of God, and is profitable. . . ."
II Timothy 3:16

The Scriptures are most surely profitable. They have been of benefit to men and women for as long as they have existed. Again and again the Bible has brought salvation, health and guidance. However, the benefit of the Word of God goes beyond this. It is effective for **every need and want of mankind.**

Back-Breaking Load of Debt

One of the greatest needs the Church faces today is release from its back-breaking load of debt. By the Church, I mean the individual members as well as the corporate structure. Debt is rampant in our midst.

Getting You Through, Not Out

The Church is hearing more prophecy than it has ever heard about the approaching end of the age. Personally, I have been hearing this message for over thirty years. I am convinced that the second coming of Christ is closer than it has ever been. However, it is evident that this event has not yet taken place.

This fact has caused me to begin to emphasize God's ability **to get us through** the everyday problems of life. For this reason, I have dedicated my ministry to prophesying **the solutions** God has for His people in these last days.

Please do not misquote me! I believe Jesus has the **ability** to return **at any moment.** Personally, I hope He does come soon. However, if He chooses to tarry His coming, I want the children of God to know that the answer to Satan's end-time strategy of debt is **God's miracle of debt cancelation!**

Today Is Not the Day of Miracles

Now I can just hear someone saying, "Why, Brother John, don't you know we live in New Testament times? God would never perform a miracle of debt cancelation in these days. Haven't you been told that **this is not the day of miracles?**

I must agree. I do not believe in the day of miracles either. However, I do believe in the **God** of miracles, and there have always been people who believe He is able to perform miracles in **the time of their need.** Miracles do not depend upon a **day** for their manifestation. They depend upon the **ability of God**, who performs them.

However, even those who willingly accept the fact that God still performs miracles often resist the possibility that He will still perform the miracle of debt cancelation.

It Serves Them Right

Many Christians feel that those who are in hopeless debt situations **deserve** the misery they have brought upon themselves. Deliverance for irresponsibility somehow seems wrong. Why, miraculous debt cancelation would be nothing more than letting the spend-thrifts have their cake and eat it too! Those who have carefully budgeted their money just don't think it is fair for those who have purchased every **impulse** item they desire to get off **scot-free**. They, of all people, **justly deserve** the hard times their reckless spending has brought upon them. Surely they should not be let off the hook with a miracle!

The Elder Brother Spirit

This is the same spirit that overcame the elder brother of the Prodigal Son. He was not disturbed because his brother had squandered all his inheritance. He was angry because his wayward brother did not have to suffer long and hard for his indiscretions.

Please let me warn you. You must guard your heart against this kind of thinking. Remember, the deliverance of God is **always unmerited**. The spirit of jealousy that results from this kind of thinking **is no better than the spirit of debt it condemns!**

No One Is Cheated When God Delivers

When a person is healed of cancer, you never hear anyone complaining, "Well, that miracle just isn't right. The doctors got cheated out of their surgical bills." You don't hear anyone saying the hospital was cheated out of their medical charges. No one says an injustice was done to the mortuary because the healing kept them from getting their fee. No one will claim that others with cancer were cheated because they were not healed.

Well, I know this thinking must sound pretty ridiculous, but I suspect these are the types of thoughts that keep most Christians from rushing to God for debt relief. Inwardly, they believe they deserve the devastation their debt has brought with it.

God Does Not Want To Give You What You Deserve

Child of God, think of it! Every lost person deserves to go to hell. Everyone has sinned and come short of the glory of God. Many people are sick because they have abused their bodies. Those who have smoked two packs of cigarettes a day have surely earned their emphysema. The vast majority of those who are in prison deserve their sentences. However, God is daily working miracles for these same, undeserving people. I never hear anyone say, "Oh! That person deserved cancer!" or "That person deserves to go to hell!"

No one **earns** salvation. No one **earns** healing. No one **earns** God's love. All God's gifts are freely given to those who have faith to receive them. In just this way, the miracle of canceled debt is freely given. **God wants to perform it because He loves you!**

It Is Not a Religious-Sounding Miracle

We seem to eagerly accept the miracle of salvation in the lives of the grossest sinners. We openly rejoice when those who have abused their health are miraculously healed.

Then, no matter what the circumstances are that bring someone into debt's clutches, why not accept a miracle of debt cancelation?

When we see a man pictured in an evangelistic magazine with his crutches lifted up toward heaven, we say to ourselves, "Isn't Jesus wonderful? Surely this proves that God still works miracles. He is a good God, for He is **the same yesterday, today, and forever."**

When we see the flowing tears of a small child who was once blind and can now see, we quickly say, "Isn't Jesus wonderful? He still works miracles. He is a good God, for He is **the same yesterday, today, and forever."**

You see, healing is a miracle we can easily identify with God. But the fact that the Church does not want to hear what the Bible says about money has made God's financial miracles sound **carnal.**

Child of God, please let it settle into your spirit once and for all. Our God does **more** than open blind eyes. He does **more** than make crippled limbs straight. He does **more** than renew the rotting flesh of the leper. **He also cancels the debts of His people!**

Please **add** the fact that God can cancel debt to your list of miracles, for He is **the same yesterday, today, and forever!** He has saved before, He has healed before, and He has delivered from the power of debt before.

If you have a debt today, your God can perform a debt-release miracle today. Whatever He did for those in the past, He can do for you in the present. Miracles are available **any day that a child of God has the faith to believe for them.**

More Qualified

I must point out another special truth to my readers. Today, you are actually more qualified to receive the miracle of canceled debt than anyone mentioned in Scripture. The Word of God clearly promises this.

After the writer of Hebrews carefully stated the miraculous way in which God moved in the lives of the Old Testament saints, he boldly promised that **something much better is available for us.**

"God having provided some better thing for us. . . ."
Hebrews 11:40

As marvelous as any miracle in the Bible may seem to you, you have a **scriptural promise of an even better miracle!**

Now, please keep this in mind. The miracle of debt release will not happen because I say it will. It will happen because **the Holy Bible, the perfect Word of God, says it will.**

". . . let God be true, but every man a liar. . . ."
Romans 3:4

Your miracle of canceled debt can be better **because** you are in a **better relationship with God through a better covenant.**

Remember, miracles are not given out by man. They are always **given by God.** They are almost never given to those who doubt that they can have them. They are given to those who **receive them through unwavering faith.**

". . . let him ask in faith, nothing wavering. . . ."
James 1:6

This can be taken one step further. Just because a desired miracle does not manifest itself immediately, that does not mean it is not available. When healing does not immediately manifest itself, you do not stop believing that the miracle of healing exists.

The same is true for the miracle of debt cancelation. After you have prayed for it, just continue to do everything in your power to pay off your debt. Keep believing, and keep praying. The miracle will take place.

Through the power of faith and patience, God **can** and **does** intervene in our lives to **miraculously** heal. In that same way, through the power of faith and patience, He will also **miraculously** intervene to help you pay your debts.

> **". . . be . . . followers of them who through faith and patience inherit the promises."**
> **Hebrews 6:12**

No circumstance is too difficult for God. He can save; He can heal; He can also break **the death grip of debt** off your life!

You Have Already Manifested Your Greatest Faith

Whenever faith is mentioned, most Christians immediately think of some great, mystical task they must perform to get God moving. Let me set your mind at ease. If you are saved, **you have already manifested enough faith** to receive the greatest miracle possible — **the miracle of salvation**.

Yes, when you received your salvation by faith, you received the greatest miracle God has to offer. No miracle can ever be greater than the miracle of new life in Jesus Christ.

Now, I must point out that some strange process takes place in most Christians soon after they accept Jesus as their Savior. With the passing of time, they grow weaker in faith instead of stronger. They begin to struggle with the miracle of healing. They struggle with the miracle of restoration of family relationships. They struggle with the miracle of increase in their finances.

Unbelief and Traditions Weaken Your Faith

For a long time I was puzzled at this strange phenomenon. Then I realized that **unbelief** and **traditions** work in direct opposition to the Christian's ability to receive.

How Unbelief Begins

Child of God, please wake up to this biblical truth. **Unbelief will restrict the miracle-working power of God in your life.**

> **"And he did not many mighty works there because of their unbelief."**
> **Matthew 13:58**

I am convinced that unbelief begins with **amazement**. When we are amazed by the miracle power of God as He moves among men, we are damaging our faith. Each time we allow amazement to manifest itself, unbelief is given an open door to enter into our spirits.

When God moves in great power, our reaction should be the exact opposite of amazement. We should actually only be amazed when He does not move. We should be amazed when a broken home we have faithfully prayed for is **not restored!** We should be amazed when the financial needs of a dedicated Christian family are **not met!**

Think about it. **Unbelief finds it roots in amazement!**

When you were a child, you were amazed by the huge airplanes your father took you to see at the airport. It seemed to you as if an impossible event had taken place when they ascended into the heavens like mighty, iron birds. But now that you are older and understand the nature of God's physical laws, the flight of an airplane **no longer leaves you in amazement**. You simply get on board, and **expect** the airplane to rise into the air because you know it can. The truth of the matter is that the whole nation actually gasps in amazement when an airplane **crashes**, not when it takes off.

Amazement comes from not understanding the nature of a thing. For instance, if you knew the professional techniques a magician used to create the illusion of sawing someone in half, your amazement at the trick would immediately cease.

Your amazement at God's movements comes from a lack of understanding of His true nature. When you fully understand God's nature, you will no longer stand amazed at His mighty miracles. You will understand that they are part of His normal activity.

Now, do not misunderstand what I have said to you. We should always remain in reverence, even in wonder, of God's sacred miracles. **But not amazement!** God can do anything the Bible says He can. Behold the wonder of His power! Thank Him for His miraculous intervention in your life! But do not be amazed, for unbelief finds it's roots in amazement. It has no place in the mind of the Child of God who knows His Lord's abilities.

> **"Is any thing too hard for the Lord? . . ."**
> **Genesis 18:14**

This verse asks a question that always brings a thunderous "No!" Yet, we still tend to be amazed when we hear that God has dissolved a cancer, stopped an addiction, or changed the heart of a wayward child.

All of these miracles are easy for God to perform. Our Bible tells us He will do even **greater things** than those which are recorded in His Word.

> **"Now unto him that is able to do exceeding abundantly above all that we ask or think, according to the power that worketh in us."**
> **Ephesians 3:20**

The power that works in us to receive miracles is not amazement, but **faith**. God can do anything!

When you fully understand God's divine nature, your **amazement will change to expectation,** for God's nature is unchanging.

"Jesus Christ the same yesterday, and to day, and
for ever."
Hebrews 13:8

When your amazement turns to expectation, **it has
turned to faith.** Faith is what expectation is made of.

"Now faith is the substance [raw material] of things
hoped for [expected], the evidence of things not
seen."
Hebrews 11:1

How Traditions Weaken Your Faith

How very powerful the Word of God is! It has turned
the course of history many times. It has guided con-
querors. It has doomed infidels. Its power is **almost**
without earthly parallel. Notice I said **"almost,"** for no
matter how powerful the Word of God is, there is a power
on planet Earth that will render its promises invalid to you.
**It is the power of any tradition you hold that is contrary
to the Word of God.**

"...Thus have ye made the commandment of God
of none effect by your tradition."
Matthew 15:6

Traditions have an unfair advantage over Christians,
for they come to us disguised as truth. The very people
who loved us enough to bring us to Christ are usually the
ones who introduce us to the traditions we receive and
defend. No matter how sacred these teachings are, if they
don't find their basis in the true interpretation of God's

Word, **they must be forsaken**. You cannot move into God's best until you reject religion's best, your traditions.

God Is Stirring a Miracle for You

I feel a miracle beginning to stir in the spirit world for you. Your traditional lifestyle of debt, with its bondage to banks, department stores, and financial institutions, has **made a slave out of you!** This day, **the tradition of being in debt begins to crumble.** God's truth about debt is beginning to flood your spirit. You now know what debt has done to you. It has made you into a servant.

> "... the borrower is servant to the lender."
> **Proverbs 22:7**

Oh, I have wonderful news for you! The miracle that will break the spirit of debt is on its way. In short order this miracle will bring you to the end of debt's domination. You are about to be set free. The revelation you are receiving from God's Word is leading you out of bondage.

Do not give way to fear. Breaking the power of debt in your life will not be too difficult for you to accomplish. You will be able to take hold of it **by your faith**. Now it will be possible for the Holy Spirit of God to lead you step by step into total debt relief.

Just promise yourself that you will not allow your **traditions** to make the Word of God of no effect. Promise yourself that you will not allow **unbelief** to weaken your faith. If you will help in this way, it will be much easier for God to release you into your new debt-free lifestyle.

Say the following sentence out loud right now.

"I am debt free through the miracle power of God!"

Say it several more times. Say it until it ceases to amaze you when you hear it. By doing this, you are kicking the bad seeds of tradition and unbelief out of your spirit. You are replacing them with the good seed of God's Word.

Remember, God's miracle of canceled debt is the property of those who are able to believe Him for it.

In the following chapter, you will learn more about the widow whose debt was miraculously canceled. Keep your **faith** focused on the **God of miracles**, and you will see that He can also perform the miracle of debt cancelation for you!

8

The Widow's Debt Was
Miraculously Canceled

". . . Go, sell the oil, and pay thy debt. . . ."
II Kings 4:7

I want to draw your attention to the widow woman I mentioned in chapter one. She faced an impossible financial situation. It was the direct result of uncontrollable debt. Her husband had just died, leaving her with the creditor at her door. However, even in the eleventh hour, she was able to receive the miracle of canceled debt.

> **"Now there cried a certain woman of the wives of the sons of the prophets unto Elisha, saying, Thy servant my husband is dead; and thou knowest that thy servant did fear the Lord: and the creditor is come to take unto him my two sons to be bondmen."**
> **II Kings 4:1**

Good People Get Into Debt

The first thing this portion of Scripture makes clear is that **if you are in debt, it does not mean you do not love the Lord.** Many Christians point the finger at each other and claim, "If that family really loved God, they would not be having such a struggle with their finances."

Nonsense! The widow's deceased husband was an associate minister of the great prophet, Elisha. He was a true servant of God! Scripture says **he feared** the Lord!

However, through ignorance or poor money management, he chose to operate in the world's debt system instead of God's debt-free system. This error in judgment brought his widow face to face with a staggering financial dilemma.

A Much Different Day Than Today

Please remember, this woman did not live in the day and age in which you live. She could not go down to the local rehabilitation center and learn some basic business skills such as typing and filing. No, she lived in an agricultural society where women were dependent upon the males in their families for their financial support. When a woman of that day found herself without husband or sons, she was on her way to the streets to beg.

Debt Is Never Considerate of Your Circumstances

I am sure it was not the intention of her husband to leave his family in financial trouble. However, it happened just the same. If you die an untimely death, your debt will not just go away. It will be inherited by your family. The husband had used his two sons as collateral, and now they would become the creditor's servants if the note was not paid in full.

I can hear someone saying, "Why, Brother John, that just doesn't seem right. She needed those two sons more than the creditor did."

That may be true. But remember, **it is debt, not fairness, that rules**! No matter what you have planned, debt has the right to overrule your plans. With the death of her husband, this poor woman was rudely awakened to the fact that debt has no regard for a person's circumstances.

The Man of God or Debt Consolidation

The biblical account makes it sound as if the widow had another option. She could have gone to the creditor one more time for help. She could have said, "Sir, give me a one-year extension, and I will pay the entire debt. Consolidate my loan, and if I cannot pay it all, **I, too, will become your bond-servant**."

Thank God this woman had more sense than that! Instead of taking this course of action, she wisely decided to go to her trusted man of God. She made a quality decision to believe that her God would break the power of debt from her life.

Supernatural, Not Natural Help

Notice that she did not approach Elisha for help from the church's **benevolent fund**. She did not come to see if the church could **co-sign** a debt consolidation loan for her.

She came to her man of God for the **divine intervention of God into her financial crisis!**

Hear Elisha's reply to her need:

> "... What shall I do for thee? tell me, what hast thou in the house? And she said, Thine handmaid hath not any thing in the house, save a pot of oil.
>
> Then he said, Go, borrow thee vessels abroad of all thy neighbours, even empty vessels; borrow not a few.
>
> And when thou art come in, thou shalt shut the door upon thee and upon thy sons, and shalt pour out into all those vessels, and thou shalt set aside that which is full.
>
> So she went from him, and shut the door upon her and upon her sons, who brought the vessels to her; and she poured out.
>
> And it came to pass, when the vessels were full, that she said unto her son, Bring me yet a vessel. And he said unto her, There is not a vessel more. And the oil stayed.
>
> Then she came and told the man of God. And he said, Go, sell the oil, and pay thy debt, and live thou and thy children of the rest."
>
> II Kings 4: 2-7

The Key to Her Miracle

The key to this miracle is that the widow was able to **trust her man of God!** Her trust in him was made evident when she told him of her only remaining asset. It was nothing more than a little pot of oil.

I can hear her two teenage boys saying, "Mama, don't tell the man of God about our little pot of oil. Mama, you know what will happen. He'll take it from us! Remember, **all preachers want is your money!**"

I can hear her answer, "Son, use your head. When you were dying with the fever, it wasn't the creditor who was down on his knees praying for your recovery. It was our man of God. He was up all night with you. Our only hope is a miracle, and he is the one who can bring it to us."

As the miraculous multiplication of oil began, I can hear her sons speak their human wisdom once again. "Mama, let's hide a few barrels of oil before the man of God sees how much we have. Mama, please remember! **All preachers want is your money!** If you tell him about it, he will take our oil for himself."

Thank God she did not listen. She knew God had great men and women serving Him. She knew they were not in God's service to take advantage of the poor. She knew the prophet's interest would be in her well-being, not his own.

The Man of God Asked for Nothing

See the reward she received for trusting in her man of God. When the miracle was complete, Elisha told her to sell the oil and **pay off her debt**. He said she and her children were to live off that which was left over. Not only was her debt paid in full, but God had a bonus for her. He also funded her retirement with this miracle.

". . . and live thou and thy children of the rest."
II Kings 4:7

Trusting the man of God is not always an easy thing to do. Let me illustrate this from my own experience. My programs are seen daily on over six hundred Christian television stations. More than 960 municipalities hear me speak on biblical economics four times every day. It is estimated that as many as five million people a day see my program. I have personally written more books on the subject of biblical economics than any other author. I am considered by most to be an expert in this field. But the truth of the matter is that **even with these credentials, I cannot help most Christians with their financial problems.** The reason may surprise you! It is because the average Christian **does not trust the man of God when it comes to their money!**

The Devil Knows Something Most of Us Don't Know

The devil knows something about biblical economics that most Christians do not know. Contrary to popular opinion, I am convinced that he is a very careful Bible student. He knows exactly what the Word of God has to say about you and the power God has given you. The devil knows that as long as you have doubt in your mind about your man of God, **you cannot operate in the prosperity of God.**

I am not just giving you my opinion on this matter. What I am saying is exactly what the Word of God says:

> "And they rose early in the morning, and went forth into the wilderness of Tekoa: and as they went forth, Jehoshaphat stood and said, Hear me, O Judah, and ye inhabitants of Jerusalem; Believe in the Lord your God, so shall ye be established; believe his prophets, so shall ye prosper."
>
> **II Chronicles 20:20**

Notice the two prerequisites to receiving the benefits of this verse.

The first one is: Believe in the **Lord your God**, so shall you be **established**. As a whole, this prerequisite is being met by the Church. We believe God, and this has brought forth an **established** membership.

For instance, if I were so foolish as to try to teach that Jesus was not born of a virgin, you would immediately throw this book in the trash. If I were to be found preaching that Jesus Christ was not coming again, you would do the same. If I were to write that the Bible was not the inspired Word of God, my publisher would immediately cease to distribute my books. If I tried to teach that your salvation was not by grace, you would not listen to me.

The reason the Church of our day would react in this way is because they **believe** the Lord their God. Consequently, they are **established**!

". . . Believe in the Lord your God, so shall ye be established. . . ."

II Chronicles 20:20

The second prerequisite is: Believe the **prophets**, so shall you **prosper**. In this point, it is painfully evident that the devil has done a great deal of damage to the Church. The membership is not walking in the prosperity they need. Not trusting the prophets has most surely taken its toll. It has put the Body of Christ outside the financial prosperity God intended.

The Greatest Miracle

You have heard many messages about the miracle of the poor widow's oil being multiplied. You have heard how great our God is because of His ability to multiply a little pot of oil into many gallons. Everybody seems to focus on that most obvious part of the story.

But I want to emphasize that this is not the biggest miracle I see here. The multiplication of olive oil takes place every year. It is so common that God does not treat it as a special event. He has simply programmed it into the cycle of nature. Nature automatically multiplies all the world's olive oil every year. There has never been a year that it hasn't happened.

No, I must say that there is a much greater miracle here. It is so understated that most would miss it if I did not emphasize it. The greatest miracle I find in this passage is that the widow **trusted her man of God with the last thing of value she possessed!**

". . . believe his prophets, so shall ye prosper."
II Chronicles 20:20

From my observation of most Christians, **that degree of trust was a big miracle!**

Remember, the devil knows that as long as he can keep you from trusting your man of God, he has effectively blocked the prosperity of God from operating in your life.

This is only one of many examples of canceled debt found in the Bible. There are several others we will be discussing in this book. In each case, trusting the man of God was of utmost importance in receiving the miracle. It will be just as important in your life.

9

All Preachers Want Is Your Money

" . . .believe his prophets, so shall ye prosper."
II Chronicles 20:20

"**All preachers want is your money!**" How often we have heard these words! I am sure you have heard them time and again. You may have even said them yourself.

Let me ask you a very important question. Have you ever heard the statement, "**All the cereal manufacturers want is your money.**"? Probably not. Yet, if you do not believe that's all they want, consider this simple test.

Think about what would happen if the next time you were in a grocery store you picked up a box of your favorite breakfast cereal, went to the check-out counter and told the clerk, "I'm not going to pay for this box of cereal. I'm taking it because all the cereal manufacturers really want is for me to have a nice, wholesome breakfast. Good-bye."

If you tried that, you would probably end up in a mental institution or in jail. (Please don't try it.)

Why don't you ever hear that all the grocer wants is your money? Why don't you hear that all the automobile dealer wants is your money? . . . all the fast food outlets want is your money? . . . all the filling stations want is your money? . . . all insurance salesmen want is your money?

All the Savings and Loan Industry Wants Is Your Money

As we have all read in the past few years, numerous institutions in the savings and loan industry have deceived their clients. They have pumped out reams of falsified documents. They have under-secured loans. Almost every rule of ethical conduct that guides their industry has been broken. All of this has resulted in many allegations of apparent fraud. It has led to the closure of countless savings institutions. These businesses were organized for one primary purpose, and one primary purpose alone — **to get your money!**

These same savings and loan associations have cost the taxpayers **billions** of dollars, yet I have not heard a single person say, **"All the savings and loan industry wants is your money."**

If for some reason you don't think the primary purpose of the savings and loan industry is to get your money, just call up your friendly banker at 2:00 a.m. Ask him if he'll run right over to your house to pray for your sick child. He will quickly let you know that his only interest in you is your money. He will probably suggest that you call a preacher if you want **free prayer** for your child.

Take my word for it, you will never find the life-saving message of the Gospel through your bank. You will not find it packaged in a six-pack of your favorite soda pop.

No fast-food chain will ever serve you the vital food you need for your eternal soul.

So why are we always hearing that it is the preachers who want our money? It is obvious that it is **everyone** else in the **world who wants our money!**

A Plot from Hell Uncovered

If you will only think about it a bit, you will have to conclude there is a sinister plot against preachers. It is specifically designed to break people's trust in the integrity of the men of God. You had better wake up to the fact that the devil is tampering with your mind! He knows if he can deceive you into believing that all preachers want is your money, it will effectively block the manifestation of God's prosperity from your life. He knows if he can do that, God will not be able to release you from the grip of insufficiency.

A Limited Devil

Many Christians do not realize that the devil's power is limited. He has only three primary powers — the power to **tempt,** the power to **accuse,** and the power to **deceive.** Of these three abilities, the power to deceive is probably his greatest weapon.

Deception is Satan's major defense against the prosperity of God's children. By deception he has convinced Christians not to trust their men and women of

God. He has done this with a master stroke of advertising genius — a one-line slogan, or better said, a **"one-lie slogan."** This now famous one-liner says, **"All preachers want is your money."** The devil knows that as long as the Church goes without prosperity, the world will not be evangelized with the Gospel of Jesus. **It takes money to reach the world.**

Prosperity Is Taught In the Bible

How is it that we can study the inspired Word of God and not realize how often it speaks of money? In one out of every six verses, the Bible talks of money or something that can be turned into money. Why is it that when we tell our pastors we want to hear the whole counsel of God we hear so few messages on the subject of money? It is because no matter how seldom our pastors preach about money, most Christians feel it is discussed too much. This attitude toward money has intimidated the men of God. It has caused them to speak less and less about this most necessary subject.

The devil is having his way in our pulpits when it comes to financial matters. He has us believing that our men and women of God are only in it for the money.

Pastors Are Valuable Assets

Do you really think your pastor could not make more money in the secular world than he makes at your church? I know thousands of pastors, evangelists, and Bible teachers. Most of them could immediately be employed by the nation's leading companies as salesmen, or even as managers. Many of them could go right into top management and receive top pay and benefits if all they wanted was money.

The reason the vast majority of preachers serve God is not for the money. It is because God has called them, and they are obedient to that call!

Those six words, "*all preachers want is your money,*" have all but stopped financial abundance in the lives of God's children. In not believing the men of God, the Church has placed itself outside the reach of His prosperity. Remember! The Bible confirms this fact.

> "... believe his prophets, so shall ye prosper."
> **II Chronicles 20:20**

If we must believe the prophets to prosper, then it stands to reason that **if we do not believe the prophets, we will not prosper.** Child of God, please remember that Satan is the father of lies, and everything he speaks is a lie. He is the one who says we cannot trust our men of God. He wants to stop you from following the biblical process that will release your God-promised prosperity.

Statistics Prove Satan Is a Liar

Just notice how untrue Satan's lie about preachers really is. Statistics prove that the statement, "*all preachers want is your money,*" *is not founded in fact.*

There are at least 700,000 churches in America today. In the last few years, out of these 700,000 institutions, there has only been one major scandal concerning a preacher and the misuse of finances. Yet, this incident has been used by the devil as proof to the world that preachers are not to be trusted with finances.

Think about it. There has been only one publicized scandal out of the 700,000 possibilities! In fraction form, this ratio would be 1/700,000. In decimal form, it would be .0000014!

699,999 Not Indicted

Let's be honest. What about the 699,999 preachers who were not accused of misusing funds during that time? Their testimony is a monument to the fact that preachers want much more *for* you than they want *from* you!

Why, the recent failures of hundreds of savings and loan associations make bankers seem like modern-day Billy-the-Kids in comparison to the few preacher scandals that take place from time to time. Yet, more money than ever is being entrusted to bankers, even though hundreds of them are being indicted and convicted of fraud on an almost daily basis.

I say it again. The Church is being deceived. Mistrust of God's men and women is rampant. This situation can never be attributed to the presently publicized scandal.

There is something much greater than a failed preacher or two behind this hellish campaign.

Don't Be Ridiculous

Let me show you how ridiculous it is to believe that all preachers want is your money. Suppose you said to me, "Brother John, I want you to come and meet a friend of mine," and I rudely responded, "I don't want to meet any friend of yours."

With great surprise, you would surely ask me why. What would you think if I very coldly stated that I make it a habit never to meet anyone's friends? After asking me how I could ever set such a ridiculous rule in my life, I would explain to you. "Well, a fellow I know down in Dallas had me meet a friend of his once. That friend ended up cheating me out of a lot of money. So now, I make it an iron-clad rule never to meet anyone's friend, because all friends will cheat you out of your money."

My reasoning would obviously be flawed. You would probably laugh at me if I were so paranoid as to actually believe that **every** friend to whom I would ever be introduced would cheat me out of my money.

Yet, that's the same kind of lie the devil is telling the Church about their men and women of God! Just because a few preachers have failed to properly perform their financial responsibility, many Christians believe that no preacher can be trusted with money.

Please do not let the devil trick you into being as ignorant as my illustration would have shown me to be. Take your men of God **one at a time.** Evaluate each one on the basis of his ministry and integrity. That is the proper way to decide whether or not you can trust him.

Your Man of God's Motive

Many of God's children are afraid to give anything to the man of God, because they do not understand his motive.

Let me give you an illustration. Suppose you are just a few days from bankruptcy. You read in the paper that I am speaking in your area. You call your pastor and ask him to bring me over to your house, so I can try and help you with your financial dilemma.

When I come in, you start to tell me that you are now in bankruptcy court, and your creditors are about to take **everything.** At that point, just suppose I walk into another room and begin to question you. "Is this television set included in the bankruptcy?"

"Yes, Brother John, it is. **Everything** I own is in the bankruptcy."

With your answer, I immediately go into another room, and ask, "How about this couch? Is it included in the bankruptcy?"

By now you become a bit irritated with me and are beginning to think that inviting me over might not have been such a good idea. You answer anyway, "Yes, Brother John, watch my lips. **Everything** in this home is involved in the bankruptcy. Why are you asking about all this stuff. Are you trying to **embarrass me?** Please, Pastor, would you and Brother John just leave? He isn't working out at all like I thought he would."

Instead of leaving, I shout a quick promise. "Just give me another minute! I'm sure I am going to be able to help you!" I run into the family room and discover something else. It is a beautiful piano. Immediately I ask, "Hey, is this piano included in the bankruptcy?"

Then I hear the reply I have been waiting for. "As a matter of fact, Brother John, **it is not**. It was given to us after the banker took an inventory of all our belongings to secure our bank note. It is the only thing we own that is not part of the bankruptcy. It is **our only unmortgaged possession.**"

"Great," I reply! "I've got the solution to your financial problem. You must **immediately sell this piano and give all the money** you receive for it **into the ministry!**"

Now, I can hear you thinking, "Why, that slimy, no-good, preacher! He'd steal the pennies right off a dead man's eyes! Why, this proves that what people say about preachers must be true. All they really want is your money!"

You Missed the Point

If this would be your reaction, you have missed the point. Giving God the money from the sale of the piano would be **essential** to having God help you overcome the financial crisis that you faced. This is not because God needs your money. It is because giving money *to* God is necessary if you hope to receive money *from* God. The Bible teaches from cover to cover that you must give to God that which you hope to receive back from Him.

> "Give, and it shall be given unto you; good measure, pressed down, and shaken together, and running over, shall men give into your bosom. For with the same measure that ye mete withal it shall be measured to you again."
>
> **Luke 6:38**

"It"

Notice the word "it." The Bible says, "Give, and **it** (that which you have given) will be given back to you." In biblical economics, to receive what you need, you must give **it**. Don't let that statement throw you. God's way of doing things is not like our way of doing things.

> "For my thoughts are not your thoughts, neither are your ways my ways, saith the Lord."
>
> **Isaiah 55:8**

Everyone knows that when you face bankruptcy, you need **money**. Nothing else will do. According to the Word of God, if **money** is what you need, then it is **money** that you must give away. Giving the sales price of the piano into the ministry would **not be an act of charity.** It would be **an act of faith.** It would be faith in God's promise to give back to you many times more than you gave to Him.

Why the Man of God Takes Offerings

If you are ever going to receive from God, you must understand the purpose of the man of God in the offering. His purpose is **not to take from you,** but to **receive for God** from you. Until this happens, it is not possible for you to **receive from God.**

No single truth is more essential to the return of Jesus Christ than that His children learn how to receive *from* God by giving *to* God. Taking the Gospel of the Kingdom to all the nations of the world is totally dependent upon Christians giving into the Gospel ministry. Without this faithful giving, the second coming of Christ will only be delayed further.

> **"And this gospel of the kingdom shall be preached**
> **in all the world for a witness unto all nations; and then**
> **shall the end come."**
> **Matthew 24:14**

There cannot be a worldwide spread of the Gospel unless abundant finances are released into the hands of God's children. They can then put those same finances into the ministries of God. This will give men and women of God the ability to go into the regions beyond and tell every creature that Jesus is the Christ, the Son of the living God, and He wants to save them.

We Gladly Tell All to the Banker

Let me interject an interesting thought. It will reveal the sad state of mistrust that exists between the Church and their men of God. To get a loan from the neighborhood bank, even the most trusted customer must reveal his complete financial statement. He must list every single asset and debt he has. Before he is allowed to come into the financial bondage of a bank, he must trust the banker and tell him all!

But not many Christians would be willing to show a complete financial statement of their assets to their pastor. Something inside us says that if the man of God knows too much about our finances, he will somehow take them away from us. Something is very wrong when we will trust the man of the world more than we trust the man of God. Everyone knows the benefits of God and His local church are far more valuable than any benefit you might receive from the bank. Yet, for some mysterious reason, we do not want the preacher to know anything about our money.

"Don't You Dare Tell Pastor!"

I have proof that what I am saying to you is true. Several years ago, when I was still in the pastorate, a little girl came up to me and said, "Brother John, can you keep a secret?"

I said, "Yes, I can keep a secret."

"You promise?"

"Yes, I promise."

With this promise secured, she began to tell me that her mother had just inherited a large amount of money. Her mother had said if the little girl told me about it, she would spank her.

This actually happened; it is a true story.

Now, this same lady who had deliberately avoided telling me about her good fortune went to her unsaved banker and said, "Look what I've got!"

She revealed her newly gained inheritance to him, and he said, "Oh, this is too good for a secured certificate of deposit. Your money won't grow nearly fast enough in that kind of an investment. We are going to put your money into a very special business venture. A new shopping center is coming to our city. Put your inheritance into that project. Trust me. All I want is for you to prosper."

Six months later, this same lady was in my office, brokenhearted and crying. "Oh, Brother John, my inheritance is completely gone. I've lost every cent of it."

Ten Percent Saved Meant One Hundred Percent Lost

Child of God, listen to me. This woman's mistrust of her man of God did save her **the ten percent tithe** that was due on the inheritance. After all, she was "smart" enough to know that, "*all preachers want is your money.*" So with this lie of the devil in her heart, she went down to her friendly banker, whose only interest was to "make her rich," and in this unscriptural mindset, she lost everything she had.

Had this woman only come to me, I would have helped her give God the tithe that belongs to Him.

> "... all the tithe of the land, whether of the seed of the land, or of the fruit of the tree, is the Lord's: it is holy unto the Lord."
> **Leviticus 27:30**

The Bible says that by tithing, she would have opened the windows of heaven over her finances.

> "Bring ye all the tithes into the storehouse ... and prove me now herewith ... if I will not open you the windows of heaven ...."
> **Malachi 3:10**

Had this woman tithed, it would have **protected** her money from those who took her inheritance.

". . . I will rebuke the devourer for your sakes. . . ."
Malachi 3:11

How foolish it is to fall for the devil's one-liner, *"all preachers want is your money."* With this information, I hope you will purge your mind of this Satan-inspired thought. I know from the Word of God that those who can trust their men of God will see His prosperity in their lives. The widow of Zarephath is a good example of this.

A Widow Trusted Her Man of God

The widow of Zarephath and her child were saved from starvation because she could trust her man of God. In I Kings, chapter 17, the prophet Elijah asked the widow to give him something to eat. At first she refused, for he had appeared at her home at the most untimely moment. Unknown to Elijah, he was asking the woman to give him her last bit of food!

". . . I am gathering two sticks, that I may go in and
dress it for me and my son, that we may eat it, and die."
I Kings 17:12

The very firewood she was gathering was to be used to cook her son's final meal. The drought and its resulting famine had brought her to the last tiny bit of nourishment she had. All hope was gone. There was no way in the natural realm for them to survive.

She, of all women, could have said, **"All the man of God wants is my last meal."** But the man of God wanted far more **for her** than he wanted **from her**. What he really wanted was to release a miracle supply to her that would save her life as well as his own. All that stood in the way of her miracle was her haunting **fear of insufficiency**. Elijah ministered **death to her fear, and life to her faith**. With a clear, bold voice, he said:

> ". . . Fear not: go and do as thou hast said: but make me thereof a little cake first, and bring it unto me, and after make for thee and for thy son.
>
> For thus saith the Lord God of Israel, The barrel of meal shall not waste, neither shall the cruse of oil fail . . . ."
>
> **I Kings 17:13,14**

The Greater Miracle

We all know that the miracle of the multiplied meal and oil followed. However, we must not let that dominate our thinking. There is an infinitely greater miracle that took place that day. The miracle to which I refer was that the widow could trust her man of God **with her family's last meal!**

What great confidence this dear woman must have had in her prophet! At his word, she took the very food from her son's mouth and gave it to Elijah. Oh! Thank God that the devil had not poisoned her mind with the lie that all the man of God wanted was her food.

Obeying the Man of God When You Cannot Obey God

The true strength of the widow's trust can only be fully understood when we realize that earlier, God **Himself** had commanded this widow woman to feed Elijah.

> "...I have commanded a widow woman there to sustain thee."
>
> **I Kings 17:9**

However, the woman's **fear of insufficiency** stopped her from being able to obey God's command.

Please notice the liberating truth of this story.

1. The widow knew the man of God was coming. She had been told by God to sustain him. **But being told by God was not enough.**

2. It took a **trusted man of God** to help her overcome her fear. With the words, "Fear not," her prophet encouraged her to obey her God. Only then was she able to carry out God's command.

Do you see how being able to trust her man of God was vital to her prosperity?

> "...believe his prophets, so shall ye prosper."
>
> **II Chronicles 20:20**

Why the Man of God Can Lead Us Where God Cannot

Isn't it amazing that there are things your man of God can lead you to do that God alone cannot? To understand why this is, you must realize that God has **never experienced fear**. But the man of God has **often experienced it**. Each time he overcomes fear, not only is he strengthened, but he is **better qualified** to help others who find themselves in the grip of fear.

> "... that we may be able to comfort them which are in any trouble, by the comfort wherewith we ourselves are comforted of God."
>
> **II Corinthians 1:4**

This is a key scriptural truth you cannot afford to overlook. Think about decisions we make for God. Many times they are only made after we receive the help of our trusted man of God.

We Usually Don't Obey God

Well, I can hear some say, "Brother John, I'm not like that. Whatever God says for me to do, I immediately do it."

Baloney! My twenty-six years of pastoral experience have shown me that people **do not** usually do what God tells them to do — at least not until after they hear their trusted man of God reconfirm what God has already said. It has happened that way many times in my own life.

Two Weeks of Saying "No"

Two weeks before I accepted Christ as my Savior, God was speaking to me night and day about getting saved. **I did not** submit to Him. **I argued with Him.** I resisted. I even told God that I still had many questions.

Then one Sunday night our local preacher was supposed to deliver his usual message in his nice and easy style. Instead, a young preacher-boy from the local seminary got up and preached hellfire and brimstone. Then we all sang "Just as I am" over and over while he waited for the sinners to come forward.

Finally, he looked straight at me and said, **"Are you going to come up here and get saved tonight, or am I going to have to come out there and drag you to this altar?"** With that word from the man of God, I finally did what God Himself had not been able to get me to do for the previous two weeks. **I got saved!**

Don't tell me we do what God tells us to do. **I know better!** That's why we need preachers.

Two and One-Half Years of Saying "No"

The same thing happened when God called me to preach. He had been calling me into full-time service for two and a half years, but I would not surrender.

I remember the night it all changed. Rev. Oliver B. Green was preaching that evening. In the middle of his sermon he stopped and said, "There's a man in this room that God has been calling to preach, and he won't surrender. I will give that person exactly **fifteen seconds** to get down here and surrender his life, or **I'm coming out there to get him!**"

Well, that was it. John Avanzini obeyed the man of God and started on the road to becoming a preacher.

The Key to Her Miracle

Hear me. The key to the great miracle at Zarephath was that the widow had the faith to obey her man of God.

> "... she went and did according to the saying of Elijah...."
>
> **I Kings 17:15**

The prosperity of God cannot break out in your life unless you get rid of the old "you-can't-trust-preachers" mentality. Stop wondering about your man of God. As long as you allow your mind to be dominated with doubt about him, you cannot receive God's best for your life.

> "... believe his prophets, so shall ye prosper."
> **II Chronicles 20:20**

Here is a saying worth repeating. **"All preachers want is what God wants for you!"** Try it and see if things do not get better really fast.

10

Jesus Had a Debt Miraculously Canceled

> "... thou shalt find a piece of money. ..."
> **Matthew 17:27**

Jesus owed a debt? I beg your pardon! Jesus would never be in debt!

Isn't it strange that we cannot think of our Lord and Savior being in debt? Why, that is not the proper lifestyle for the Son of God! Now, hear me as I speak to your spirit. Whatever lifestyle is not proper for our Lord is not proper for His children either. Scripture is clear on this.

> "... as he is, so are we in this world."
> **I John 4:17**

> "... we all ... are changed into the same image
> from glory to glory. ..."
> **II Corinthians 3:18**

Some Debts Are Unavoidable

Debts are incurred by everyone. Sometimes they are not the result of poor financial practices. I know Jesus conducted His business matters in a proper way. The debt

He owed was one everyone will owe. It was in the form of a tax bill.

Now, I call this a **debt** because taxes are always paid in arrears. They are never paid in advance. My wife and I are debt free, so to speak, but we have a bill that never gets paid off. It is our taxes.

Let's read what the Bible says about our Lord's miracle of canceled debt.

> **"And when they were come to Capernaum, they**
> **that received tribute money came to Peter, and said,**
> **Doth not your master pay tribute?"**
> **Matthew 17:24**

The word translated "tribute" is the Greek word that literally means "the double drachma." This was the name of the coin used to pay the temple tax. Yes, Jesus and Peter were faced with a tax bill. Notice that Simon Peter immediately told the tax collector that His master most certainly did pay taxes.

> **"He saith, Yes...."**
> **Matthew 17:25**

Surely Jesus paid taxes, for He fulfilled all righteousness. Later, Peter himself wrote that we, as Christians, should obey the laws of the land.

> **"Submit yourselves to every ordinance of man for**
> **the Lord's sake: whether it be to the king, as supreme;**
> **Or unto governors...."**
> **I Peter 2:13, 14**

Jesus said to give to the government that which belongs to the government.

> "... Render to Caesar the things that are Caesar's ...."
>
> **Mark 12:17**

Jesus Chose the Miraculous

As you look closely, you will see that Jesus actually stopped Simon Peter from paying the debt in the normal way. I believe Peter was on his way into the house to get the tax money from the treasurer, Judas. With this money, he was going to pay the tax bill for Jesus and himself.

> "... And when he was come into the house, Jesus prevented him. ..."
>
> **Matthew 17:25**

The verse tells us that Jesus stopped him from his planned action, for He had a better plan. This time the debt would not be paid from the treasury. There would be a miraculous cancelation of debt.

Jesus acknowledged the unfair way in which the taxes of this world were being taken.

> "... What thinkest thou Simon? of whom do the kings of the earth take custom or tribute? of their own children, or of strangers?"
>
> **Matthew 17:25**

Jesus asked Peter a question that dealt with how the corrupt tax system of this world operated. He asked him if he thought the king's children had to pay this tax. Simon said, "No, Lord. The strangers have to pay the tax." Jesus was showing Peter that the system controlling the world is corrupt. They tax strangers, and do not tax their own. But He quickly told Simon not to get hung up on this inequity. To keep from offending anyone and causing themselves unnecessary trouble, they would pay the tax, **but not out of the treasury.** Instead they would cancel the tax bill with a miracle.

> **"Notwithstanding, lest we should offend them, go thou to the sea, and cast an hook, and take up the fish that first cometh up; and when thou hast opened his mouth, thou shalt find a piece of money: that take, and give unto them for me and thee."**
> **Matthew 17:27**

When this event is looked at as a miraculous cancelation of debt, it makes most Christians very uncomfortable. We can easily believe the miracle of the coin being found in the fish's mouth. However, we do not like the thought that this was a debt cancelation. We especially do not like to hear that this miracle is available to Christians **today.**

He Is Always the Same

We can tolerate a God who canceled debt in the Old Testament. Why, we are even able to accept that God would cancel debt in the millennium or at His second coming. But a debt-canceling God **for today** is more than most can believe!

Once again I must say He is:

> "... the same yesterday, and to day, and for ever."
> **Hebrews 13:8**

If Jesus performed the miracle of canceled debt in the past, He will perform it in the present. Peter did nothing to **earn** the payment of that debt. Jesus did nothing to **earn** His tax money either. Both Jesus and Simon Peter were recipients of the miracle of canceled debt. By a supernatural miracle, Peter pulled a coin from the mouth of a fish. That coin was of sufficient value to pay the tax bill for both of them **in full**.

Never once did Jesus say, "Now, Peter, this is a once-in-a-lifetime miracle, so don't expect it to ever happen again."

Trust In the Man of God Was Needed

One other major point should be considered here. It is of utmost importance to your miracle of canceled debt. Although Jesus Christ was God Himself, at this time, Peter only knew Him as a man. Before the miracle could be manifested, Peter had to be willing to **believe and obey his man of God**, Jesus.

If Peter had told Jesus, "Lord, you have got to be kidding. I'm not going to go down to the sea and make a complete fool of myself by looking for money in a fish's mouth. Why, Lord. I am a fisherman. I've looked in fish's mouths countless times. I have lots of experience with fish, and I have never found a coin in one before!"

If Peter had not believed his man of God, the miraculous cancelation of the tax bill would never have taken place. Peter had a clear-cut choice. **Believe the man of God and prosper, or doubt the man of God and block the prosperity of God.**

> **". . . believe his prophets, so shall ye prosper."**
> **II Chronicles 20:20**

He chose to believe his man of God, and he prospered. The miracle of canceled debt was his. Don't you know Peter was glad he trusted his man of God when he saw his tax bill marked **paid in full**?

In this chapter we have seen another great miracle of canceled debt from the Word of God. What a blessing this is to you, for if God did it for others, He will do it for you.

> **". . . God is no respecter of persons."**
> **Acts 10:34**

11

The Children of Israel Had a Debt Miraculously Canceled

"And the children of Israel. . . borrowed of the Egyptians. . . ."

Exodus 12:35

One of the most interesting stories ever told is recorded in the book of Exodus. It is the story of a nation freed from bondage. It is so well-known, it has become the universal standard for deliverance. This example of the power of God is used by more people than any other when deliverance from impossible circumstances is described. Everyone knows about it. It transcends religious beliefs. It has been spoken of throughout the civilized world. It is so popular, Hollywood has made a famous movie about it.

I am speaking of **the exodus** of the Children of Israel. The word "exodus" has found its way into most languages. It is commonly used by many who don't even know it has a biblical origin.

A Very Real Event

While the exodus seems like a fable to many people today, it was very real to those who experienced it. Their four hundred years of slavery was a very long time. It was long enough to see the clan of Jacob grow into a nation of millions. But they were not just millions of people. They were the Children of Israel, **the blessed seed of Abraham.** They were the people of promise, for Abraham had a **covenant with God** that included his children and his children's children.

The Worst Kind of Poverty

Slavery is the very worst kind of poverty. Not only is it an existence void of all but the most meager necessities; it is dominated by the slave's ever-present knowledge that he is looked upon as nothing more than a possession himself. Plain and simple, a slave is considered to be chattel — the property of another person. A slave owns nothing except the bitterness that grows daily within his spirit. There is no poorer physical state than slavery.

A Nation Without Assets

Four hundred years of slavery had brought the nation of Israel to the brink of non-existence. Even if by some miracle they were to be liberated, they would have no assets as a nation. Without wealth, it would **only be a matter of time** before they would be trapped in slavery again. For on planet Earth, money is essential to accomplish even the simplest of tasks. Even in today's economy, a bankrupt nation soon loses its freedom, and then its identity. This principle is not only taught in world economics; it is also taught in Scripture.

> "... money answereth all things."
> **Ecclesiastes 10:19**

A Divinely Arranged Loan

As God began the deliverance of His people, He knew they would need to be properly funded. God knew that in their destitute condition, they wouldn't keep their freedom as a nation for very long.

To solve Israel's financial problem, God determined that those who had exploited them would now finance them with a loan. This loan would be necessary for Israel to set up a working government. They needed money to fund their immediate needs until enough time had passed for them to become self-sufficient. With this in mind, God instructed the women to **borrow from their Egyptian masters.**

> **"And I will give this people favour in the sight of the Egyptians: and it shall come to pass, that, when ye go, ye shall not go empty.**
> **But every woman shall borrow of her neighbour, and of her that sojourneth in her house, jewels of silver, and jewels of gold, and raiment: and ye shall put them upon your sons, and upon your daughters; and ye shall spoil the Egyptians."**
> **Exodus 3:21, 22**

Then God instructed the men to borrow from the Egyptians.

> "Speak now in the ears of the people, and let every
> man borrow of his neighbour, jewels of silver, and
> jewels of gold."
> **Exodus 11:2**

Scripture tells us that Israel willingly carried out the Lord's command.

> "And the children of Israel did according to the
> word of Moses; and they borrowed of the Egyptians
> jewels of silver, and jewels of gold, and raiment:
> And the Lord gave the people favour in the sight of
> the Egyptians, so that they lent unto them such things
> as they required. . . ."
> **Exodus 12:35, 36**

There is no possible way to calculate exactly how much wealth the children of Israel borrowed from Egypt. But Scripture gives us a hint as to the magnitude of the loan.

> ". . . And they spoiled the Egyptians."
> **Exodus 12:36**

The English word "spoil" is a translation of the Hebrew word "natsal." It is a primitive root word meaning "**to snatch away,** whether in a good or a bad sense." In the authorized version of the Bible, several very descriptive English words are used to convey its meaning.

We can see the amount borrowed was astronomical! Scripture says the Israelites spoiled (plucked, stripped) the Egyptians.

It Really Was a Loan

Many take issue with the King James translation of the word "borrowed." In the margin of some Bibles, there is a critical note that says the correct interpretation of the word should actually be "to ask for a gift." To those who lean to this interpretation, I would like to point out that the same Hebrew word is translated "borrow" in the account of the widow in the fourth chapter of II Kings. In that portion of Scripture, the prophet told her to **borrow** vessels from her neighbors.

> "... Go, borrow thee vessels abroad of all thy
> neighbours, even empty vessels; borrow not a few."
> **II Kings 4:3**

If the Hebrew word meant "to ask for a gift," it would be a very poor word to choose when instructing her to obtain as many empty vessels as she could. The meaning of the verse would drastically change if Elijah sent the widow to ask her neighbors for a "gift" of empty vessels.

The same word is again translated "borrowed" in the sixth chapter of the same book. Here it is used to describe how a young prophet had come into the possession of the ax he was using.

> "But as one was felling a beam, the axe head fell
> into the water: and he cried, and said, Alas, master! for
> it was borrowed."
> **II Kings 6:5**

If the intended meaning was "to ask for a gift," the young man would have said, "Alas, master! For I asked for it to be given to me as a gift!" Any reasonable person would immediately have to agree that the young man used a poor choice of words if this was his meaning.

The irrefutable proof as to the proper rendering of the word is established beyond a shadow of a doubt in the way Moses used it. He used this same word again and again in the book of Exodus. Here is one very plain example.

> **"And if a man borrow aught of his neighbour, and it be hurt, or die, the owner thereof being not with it, he shall surely make it good."**
> **Exodus 22:14**

When Moses used this word, he obviously meant that a person should replace something that was borrowed, not something that was a gift. If the word "natsal" meant to ask for a gift, then Moses could not say "the owner thereof being not with it." If it were a gift, it would no longer belong to the lender. If it were a gift, it would not be necessary to replace it if "it be hurt, or die."

It Was Loaned

Make no mistake about it. God told Israel to **borrow** of the Egyptians. However, there is yet one more ingredient needed before it can actually be called borrowing. If you do not have the agreement of the owner to allow you to borrow something, then you have really **taken** it, not borrowed it.

Now hear the agreement to the loan that was openly made by the Egyptians.

> **"And the Lord gave the people favour in the sight of the Egyptians, so that they lent unto them. . . ."**
> **Exodus 12:36**

With this said, it is without contradiction that a loan existed between the parties involved. There were **borrowers**, there were **things borrowed**, and there was an agreement that the things borrowed were being **loaned**.

A Nation's Debt Divinely Canceled

If this was a loan, as the Scriptures say it was, then the next question that must be answered is this. When did this loan get paid off? A gift does not call for a payoff. Property taken during wartime does not have to be returned. But a loan is an entirely different thing — especially a loan arranged by God. That type of loan must surely be repaid, unless it is canceled.

Israel's debt to Egypt was miraculously canceled in the midst of the Red Sea as the Egyptians drowned. Remember, they had given their word that Israel was free to leave. However, at the last minute, instead of releasing Israel, they pursued them into the parted sea.

Make no mistake about it. Their purpose was not to bid them farewell, but to take them back as captives. They violated their agreement with Israel and with God. When

Egypt refused to honor their side of the bargain, God canceled **all agreements with Egypt forever.**

Hear Moses as he declared the miracle of God's total release and deliverance.

> "... Fear ye not, stand still, and see the salvation of the Lord, which he will shew to you to day: for the Egyptians whom ye have seen to day, ye shall see them again no more, for ever."
>
> **Exodus 14:13**

When the Red Sea closed in over Egypt, Israel's entire national debt was canceled! In only a few hours, all of their creditors lay dead on the shore of the Red Sea. In that moment, Israel enjoyed the fullness of the word "salvation." They were free of their chains. They could worship their God as He had directed them. They were free in their **bodies.** They were no longer slaves. **They were free in their FINANCES! They were rich; and best of all, they were debt-free!**

> "Thus the Lord saved Israel that day out of the hand of the Egyptians; and Israel saw the Egyptians dead upon the sea shore.
> And Israel saw that great work which the Lord did upon the Egyptians: and the people feared the Lord, and believed the Lord, and his servant Moses."
>
> **Exodus 14:30, 31**

Total Deliverance Is Available to All

Thank God for His complete salvation! Total deliverance is available to everyone who believes on the

Lord Jesus Christ. For too long the Christian church has used a very narrow definition of God's deliverance. They have primarily interpreted it as it pertains to non-tangible matters. However, the scope of our deliverance is much greater than this. Yes, Jesus can save the **soul**. Yes, He can also heal the **body**. He can even heal the **broken hearted**. But hear this loud and clear! **He can also deliver those who have been caught in the cruel jaws of debt!**

Thank God for His total deliverance!

> **"The righteous cry, and the Lord heareth, and delivereth them out of all their troubles."**
> **Psalm 34:17**

Hear the Word of God. He delivers the righteous ("born again") out of **all** their troubles — **even their debt troubles!**

12

Other Debt Cancelations Found In God's Word

"... even the world itself could not contain the
books that should be written. ..."
John 21:25

To my knowledge, there is no reference book that lists
the debt cancelations that occur in Scripture, so it is impossible for me to say that I have found them all. Since
my study has not been exhaustive, I have no doubt that
there are other cases in the Word of God. With this in
mind, I am here recording the additional cases I have
found.

Some of King David's Men Were In Debt

In the Book of I Samuel, we are told of a group of men
who joined with David when Saul turned against him.
They were not the kind of people you would find on the
"Who's Who in Israel" list. Exactly the opposite was true.
They were the social outcasts, the malcontents, and the
candidates for bankruptcy court. We are told there were
about four hundred men, and David became their captain.

**"And every one that was in distress, and *every one
that was in debt*, and every one that was discontented,
gathered themselves unto him; and he became a captain**

over them: and there were with him about four hundred men."

I Samuel 22:2

Their struggle with King Saul went on for years. Eventually, Saul was killed, and David was made king. I have not found any direct word saying these men had their debts canceled. However, after King David came to his throne, many men from his original band of four hundred became leaders in Israel. One can easily assume that with David's ascension to the throne, the debts of those who followed him in his early years were canceled.

Nehemiah's Workmen Had Their Mortgages Canceled

In the book of Nehemiah, one of the most intensive construction projects of Scripture is recorded. The city of Jerusalem was in shambles. Much of the wall had been broken down. The gates were off their hinges. The band of men who came with Nehemiah were working night and day. In the midst of this intensive labor effort, Nehemiah found out that some of the Jews had been lending money to his workers. The biblical account describes the terrible situation these workmen had gotten into at the hands of these unscrupulous businessmen.

"And there was a great cry of the people and of their wives against their brethren the Jews.

For there were that said, We, our sons, and our daughters, are many: therefore we take up corn for them, that we may eat, and live.

> Some also there were that said, *We have mortgaged our lands, vineyards, and houses,* **that we might buy corn, because of the dearth.**
>
> **There were also that said, We have borrowed money for the king's tribute, and that upon our lands and vineyards."**
>
> **Nehemiah 5:1-4**

With this revelation, Nehemiah commanded the Jews to release the laborers from their debts and restore to them everything they had repossessed.

> **"***Restore,* **I pray you, to them, even this day, their lands, their vineyards, their oliveyards, and their houses, also the hundredth part of the money, and of the corn, the wine, and the oil, that ye exact of them."**
>
> **Nehemiah 5:11**

In obedience, the Jewish money lenders released all of Nehemiah's workers from their mortgages and restored all of their lands and possessions.

> **"Then said they, We will restore them, and will re-quire nothing of them; so will we do as thou sayest . . . ."**
>
> **Nehemiah 5:12**

A Slave Named Onesimus Had His Debt Canceled

In the book of Philemon, the Apostle Paul wrote that the runaway slave, Onesimus, had been saved under his ministry in Rome. Because Onesimus had run away, he was in debt to Philemon, his master. In the eighteenth verse, Philemon was asked to forgive the debt and charge to Paul anything the slave owed.

> **"If he hath wronged thee, or** *oweth thee aught, put that on mine account;*
> **I Paul have written it with mine own hand,** *I will repay it:* **albeit I do not say to thee how thou owest unto me even thine own self besides."**
> **Philemon 18, 19**

David's Father Had His Debt Canceled

One last account remains. It took place in the life of David's father. King Saul had promised that the father of the person who defeated Goliath would be made debt free in Israel.

> **"And all the men of Israel, when they saw the man, fled from him, and were sore afraid.**
> **And the men of Israel said, Have ye seen this man that is come up? surely to defy Israel is he come up: and it shall be, that the man who killeth him, the king will enrich him with great riches, and will give him his daughter, and make his father's house free in Israel.**
> **And David spake to the men that stood by him, saying, What shall be done to the man that killeth this Philistine, and taketh away the reproach from Israel? for who is this uncircumcised Philistine, that he should defy the armies of the living God?**
> **And the people answered him after this manner, saying, So shall it be done to the man that killeth him."**
> **I Samuel 17:24-27**

As we know, David slew the giant and collected the prize from Saul. Any debt David's father, Jesse, may have had was then canceled.

None of these debt cancelations were recorded in Scripture as miraculous events. However, anytime a debt is canceled for a child of God, it is the result of God's intervention on behalf of that faithful son or daughter. That makes every Christian's canceled debt a miracle.

For that reason, I have recorded these cases together here in this chapter. I do this in an attempt to be as thorough as I can in presenting what the Word of God says about debt release.

13

The Power of Debt Can Be Broken

"... devils are subject unto us through thy name."
Luke 10:17

Debt is a spirit, and all spirits **must leave** when they are commanded to do so in the **mighty name of Jesus!**

"Behold, I give unto you power to tread on serpents and scorpions, and over *all the power of the enemy.* ..."
Luke 10:19

"And whatsoever ye shall ask in my name, that will I do, that the Father may be glorified in the Son."
John 14:13

First, Bind the Chief Spirit

God has given us **power** in the spirit world. However, before any problem that arises from demon spirits can be solved, **the chief spirit** must be dealt with.

"... how can one enter into a strong man's house, and spoil his goods, except he *first bind the strong man?* and then he will spoil his house."
Matthew 12:29

Debt cancelation must be preceded by **putting a stop to the increase of debt.** The spirit of debt must first be

149

bound from your finances before any significant changes can be accomplished. You will find that behavior modification becomes relatively easy when the chief spirit that caused the adverse behavior is removed.

Twelve Hundred Miles from My Bills

One night a few years ago I was in a telethon in Greensville, North Carolina. God had been showing me from Scripture that there is a spirit of debt. He showed me that not only had this spirit influenced the lost, but it had also driven **most of the Christian world** into the debt lifestyle.

When I departed for the station that night, I knew that before the audience would be able to receive the full prosperity of God, the power of the spirit of debt would have to be broken off their finances. I asked the viewers to gather up their bills and bring them before their television screens. God had told me the people should have their bills in hand when I prayed. This was the first time I ever rebuked the spirit of debt.

Just before I began to pray, my wife said we also needed this release. At that moment, our own bills were almost twelve hundred miles away. How could we partake under these circumstances?

Immediately the Holy Spirit showed me a way to take the anointing of that moment back home with me to our debts. I told my wife, "Take an offering envelope, and let's hold it up in the place of our bills."

I earnestly prayed, in the name of Jesus, that the viewers who joined their faith with ours would receive a release from the spirit of debt. Then my wife and I took that very special offering envelope home with us and placed it in the midst of our bills.

Each time one of our bills was paid off, we waived the anointed envelope in the air and proclaimed that the spirit of debt had been forever broken off our lives. We also declared openly that the miracle of canceled debt had been released to us. Then we placed the anointed envelope back among our bills, speaking only that all the bills would soon be paid in full.

We continued this process for the next few years. Then one day we burned our last bill. It was the mortgage on our parsonage! This was the first time in our thirty years of marriage that my wife and I were totally debt-free.

Steps That Will Take You Out of Debt

From my own experience, I can now say that breaking the power of debt will not be nearly as hard for you as the devil would have you believe. However, there are several definite steps that must be taken for you to succeed. Please prayerfully read the following list.

1. You must sit down with a pencil and paper and list every bill you owe. This accounting must be done before you can launch a proper plan of attack against the havoc the spirit of debt has wrought in your personal finances.

This is not a secular approach to your problem. It is prescribed by our Lord Himself.

> **"For which of you, intending to build a tower, sitteth not down first, and counteth the cost, whether he have sufficient to finish it?"**
> **Luke 14:28**

Count the cost the spirit of debt has brought to your life. Recognize that he has been the motivating force behind your bills.

When you have the whole picture clearly outlined before you, ask God for the specific financial miracles you need to free you from the bondage of your debt. Remember to be thankful for any progress you make in debt reduction. Your first financial miracle may be **very small,** but acknowledge that it has come from God. Be sure to let principalities and powers know it is not your last financial miracle. There will be many more.

> **". . . faith is the substance of things hoped for. . . ."**
> **Hebrews 11:1**

If you are not acknowledging financial miracles, they will cease.

2. If at all possible, you should have a relationship with a good local church.

Why is this important? Because giving your tithes into the good ground is necessary to keep the windows of heaven open over your finances.

> **"Bring ye all the tithes into the storehouse, that there may be meat in mine house, and prove me now herewith, saith the Lord of hosts, if I will not open you the windows of heaven. . . ."**
> **Malachi 3:10**

You cannot expect to reap financial miracles unless the windows of heaven are open over your life.

3. It is also necessary to associate yourself with some good- ground ministries such as a Christian television station, a good Bible teacher, or an evangelist.

The reason this relationship is necessary is because you will need a good place to give your offerings. Your offerings will provide God with the measure He needs to pour out your financial blessings.

4. The strong man must be bound.

> **". . . how can one enter into a strong man's house, and spoil his goods, except he *first bind the strong man?* . . ."**
> **Matthew 12:29**

You must speak specifically to the strong man (the spirit of debt). Tell him he is bound from any further influence in your finances. To put it plainly, he must release his hold on your money. Bind him and cast him from your life. Be sure you do this in the mighty name of Jesus.

Remember, His name is infinitely stronger than the spirit of debt. The Bible says:

"That at the name of Jesus *every* knee should bow, of things in heaven, and things in earth, and things under the earth;"
Philippians 2:10

You are not to be afraid when you speak to the spirit of debt. **It is the spirit of debt who must be afraid.** You have something going for you that is bigger and stronger than anything the devil has going for him.

"...*greater* is *he* that is *in you,* than *he* that is *in the world.*"
I John 4:4

(I will lead you in speaking to the spirit of debt in the confession in the next step.)

5.   Now lift your bills up before the Lord, and repeat this prayer. Say it out loud.

"Dear Lord,
"I know that You care for me, spirit, soul, and body. Lord, I have many bills. They are a hindrance to me. They keep me from giving to You the way I really want to.
"Lord, I believe that Brother John is a true man of God. I believe what he has taught me about the spirit of debt is true. I believe You are concerned about my bills and that You want to help me eliminate them.

"Lord, I ask You, in the name of Jesus, to break the spirit of debt from my life. I also ask you to miraculously cancel my debt.

"Lord, I believe that as this man of God and I join our faith together, something very special is being released into my life. I thank you that you have given me authority over the entire spirit world.

"Right now, I boldly speak to the chief spirit, the spirit of debt that has been sent by the devil. In the mighty name of Jesus, I declare you to be bound. I break your hold on my life and on my finances! Spirit of debt, you can no longer operate in my life! In Jesus name, you are firmly bound, and I am loosed from your power over me!

"Father God, part the heavens for me. Let me know in my spirit that this foul spirit has been bound and defeated.

"I now speak to the East, the West, the North, the South, that the ministering angels of God come forth and begin to release the abundance of God into my life. I boldly speak that miracles must begin to take place in my finances right now. In the name of Jesus, I accept my financial breakthrough.

"Lord, I give you the glory for the financial miracles that are released into my life this day. Amen."

Say It Out Loud

Oh, Child of God, say it out loud. "The power of the spirit of debt is broken from my life this day!" Say it again and again until it rings in the devil's ears. The spirit of debt has controlled your finances for the last day.

155

If you are married, go immediately and tell your spouse that the spirit of debt has been broken from your lives. Join together in proclaiming your financial victory.

If you are single, tell the next person you meet that the spirit of debt has been broken off your life.

> **"If the Son therefore shall make you free, ye shall be free indeed."**
>
> **John 8:36**

14

You Have a Supernatural Power To Get Wealth

"... I give unto you power... over all the power...."
Luke 10:19

Up to this point you have read some truly wonderful things. However, there is still much more. God has another powerful miracle for you which is totally separate from the miracle of **canceled debt.** This miracle will help **speed** you **out of debt.**

As you read this next verse, don't resist it. Allow its full impact to be released into your spirit.

"But thou shalt remember the Lord thy God: for it is he that *giveth thee power to get wealth. ...*"
Deuteronomy 8:18

Yes, you read right! God has given you supernatural, miracle power to get wealth. This power has been made available to all the seed of Abraham. When the Word of God says something is for the seed of Abraham, that means it is available to you. **You are the seed of Abraham!**

"And if ye be Christ's, *then are ye Abraham's seed,* **and heirs according to the promise."**
Galatians 3:29

Power In Your Hands

If you carefully read Deuteronomy 8:17, you will see that the power to get wealth is given **into your hands.**

> "... the might of mine *hand* hath gotten me this wealth.
> But thou shalt remember the Lord thy God: for it is he that giveth thee power to get wealth...."
> Deuteronomy 8:17, 18

Just think about it. Your hands have been given miracle power to get wealth!

A New Confession

It is important that you begin today to make a new confession about your hands. Hold them before you right now and boldly say, **"These hands have been given supernatural power to get wealth."** Remember, the Bible says that whatever you say has a great impact on what you will have.

> "... he shall have whatsoever he saith."
> Mark 11:23

Power, Not Skill

Please don't confuse this ability with your own skill. God has given you **power, not skill**, to get wealth. God always multiplies money to His children through the miracle of the financial harvest. Miracles are always performed by the **power** of God, not by the skill of man.

Whether you are skilled or not, if you are the seed of Abraham, Deuteronomy 8:18 says you have supernatural, miracle power in your hands to get wealth. Thank God! He can bring great financial power even to the unskilled, for He gives us all **power** to get wealth.

Look at your hands again and say, "These hands have the **power** to get wealth." You should say this several times a day. You should say it until the doubt and amazement leave you, and strong faith and conviction remain.

Yes, **you have miracle power to get wealth!**

Wealth for a Purpose

The power to get wealth has been given to you for a specific purpose. God's purpose for the wealth is to establish His covenant.

> **"But thou shalt remember the Lord thy God: for it is he that giveth thee power to get wealth,** *that he may establish his covenant* **which he sware unto thy fathers, as it is this day."**
> **Deuteronomy 8:18**

When something is established, it is set and financially sound. God wants to financially establish His covenant in the earth through your power to get wealth. But before this can happen, you must understand what His covenant says.

Be a Blessing

Be careful not to let your tradition confuse you as to which covenant God is talking about. It is the one He made with Abraham.

> "And I will make of thee a great nation, and I will bless thee, and make thy name great; and *thou shalt be a blessing:*
> And I will bless them that bless thee, and curse him that curseth thee: and *in thee shall all families of the earth be blessed.*"
>
> **Genesis 12:2, 3**

The majority of Christians are continuously **seeking** the blessing. Above all else, they **want to be blessed.** Now, make no mistake about it. Being blessed by God is a wonderful thing. It is a wonderful blessing to be saved. It is just as wonderful to be filled with the Holy Spirit. It is especially wonderful to be made physically whole.

But there is a far greater calling upon the Church. There is a call of God on those who participate in the Abrahamic covenant that takes us far **beyond just being blessed, all the way to being a blessing.**

Jesus Wasn't Trying To Get Blessed

Remember, as a Christian, you have been called to be like your Savior, Jesus. He did not wander this earth seeking to be blessed. Instead, He was doing everything in His power to **be a blessing**. God has given you the power to get wealth so you can **be a blessing** to all the families of the world.

The Oppressed Await the Funding of the Church

Abraham Lincoln released the slaves, but since that release took place, there is a new kind of slavery in our land. It is not just the slavery of the black man. It also affects whites, Hispanics, and Asians. I speak of the slavery of the welfare system.

This heartless system sucks the very life out of its recipients. This great injustice goes on as the Church sits by, **helpless to do anything about it.** The reason the Church is helpless is because its members **must** pay their debts instead of properly giving into the ministry. Remember, **debt rules!**

Thank God Someone Did Something

Please do not misunderstand. I am not just blasting the welfare program. I am not advocating that there be no welfare system. Thank God someone did something! The government has done its best. But it is not God's chosen instrument to take care of the welfare of the people.

Yes, you heard me right. **It is not the job of the United States Government to meet the needs of the poor!** It is the job of the **Nation of God!** Make no mistake about it. The Church is a nation.

> "... ye are a chosen generation, a royal priesthood,
> *an holy nation,* a peculiar people...."
> **I Peter 2:9**

The Way Out of Poverty and Into Employment

When the Church is properly funded, we will be able to put forth a welfare program that will lift men and women out of poverty and into the job market. We will get families out of the ghettos. Why, the very ghettos themselves will have to go. All communities will have wonderful environments of abundance and happiness.

This is not a dream. It is possible. What we need are the funds God has allocated for the Church. Those funds must be given to the ministry, **not to the creditor!**

"Allocated funds for the Church, Brother John? I have never heard of that."

If Everyone Tithed

If every Christian in the world tithed, the Nation of God (the Church) would be the richest nation on earth. At present it is estimated that only about **eighteen percent** of the members of Bible-believing churches tithe. Just think about it. **Eighty-two percent** of the Church **is not tithing.** That means there is more than four times as much money allocated by God for the Church than it is now receiving.

All the wonderful things God has designed the Church to do are dependent upon proper funding. The finances have been held up **because once the saints are through paying the creditor,** there is only a handful of pennies left for the Church. Oh, **how harshly debt rules!**

You and Others Are Now Free!

But thank God, debt no longer rules in your life! Thank God, each day hundreds, even thousands of Christians are casting off the spirit of debt just as you have. Very soon the coffers of the Church will be full and the welfare of the poor will no longer be the work of the State. It will once again be the work of the Church. Then, and only then will the back of poverty be broken. Then will the reapers overtake the sowers. Then, and only then will the Gospel of the Kingdom of God be preached to every nation. The entire world will be evangelized.

"... thou shalt be a blessing... in thee shall all
families of the earth be blessed."
Genesis 12:2, 3

The World Has Already Been Evangelized

I have heard well-meaning people say, "Why, everyone knows the world cannot be evangelized. It is too big a job. The Church has been trying to do it for 2,000 years, and we are further from accomplishing the task than ever before."

Let me boldly say this to everyone who will hear. **World evangelism is not an impossible task!** As a matter of fact, the world has been evangelized many times. Even the most remote areas of our globe now know about Coca Cola, Mickey Mouse, Texaco, and Camel cigarettes. These companies have evangelized the world many times over.

Keep in mind that they did this without the benefit of Spirit-filled salespeople. Their products were inferior to the Gospel of Jesus Christ. The only thing these companies have that the Church does not have is **more than enough money!**

Make no mistake about it. The lost have the money, and with it they evangelize the world every day with colas, whiskey, beer, cigarettes, and cartoon characters. This proves beyond a shadow of a doubt that the Scripture is right when it says:

". . . money answereth all things."
Ecclesiastes 10:19

Don't you just know that when the power of debt is broken, the Church will have the money it needs to evangelize the world? Now is the time for Christians to get serious about reaching the nations of the world. Believe me, it is not impossible.

". . . in thee shall all families of the earth be blessed."
Genesis 12:3

Some of the Blessing Is for You

Now don't misunderstand. That doesn't mean all the wealth you receive is to be used to bless others. God wants you to have enough money to also take care of your own needs. It is to be used to get yourself out of debt, to supply your necessities of life, and even those things that are not necessities. God even wants you to have those things you desire.

"God is able to make it up to you *by giving you everything you need* **and more, so that there will not only be** *enough for your own needs,* **but plenty left over to give joyfully to others."**
II Corinthians 9:8 TLB

Let's Face Facts

You cannot **be** the blessing God has called you to be if you have not first **been** blessed. God knows you cannot properly fund His end-time harvest if you are up to your eyeballs in debt. He knows you cannot feed the hungry if you have only enough to pay the bill collector. God knows you cannot clothe the naked if every cent you have goes to pay off the clothes you are forced to buy with your credit card.

Because of this, He has provided you with supernatural miracle power in your hands to get wealth. When this is fully operational in your life, you will be able to feed the poor, clothe the naked, and fund the outreaches of your local church. Why, you will even have enough to **rapidly pay off your own debts!** The Bible actually says you will have so much there will be **more than enough** to give joyfully, not grudgingly, to others.

> "... there will not only be enough for your own needs, but *plenty left over* to give joyfully to others."
> **II Corinthians 9:8 TLB**

This great power to get wealth was not given to the Church to be wasted on **endless installment payments.** It was given to be used to wage war against the devil and his demon forces.

Two Powers Revealed

You have learned of two tremendous miracle powers in this book. You now know about **the miracle that breaks the power of debt,** and you have also learned of **your supernatural, miracle power to get wealth.** With these two gifts firmly planted in your spirit, you are now better able to receive the miracle of canceled debt in your life.

15

Where Will All This Money Come From?

" . . . the wealth of the sinner is laid up for the just."
Proverbs 13:22

By now you have probably begun to wonder where in the world you will ever get enough wealth to meet your needs, **plus** enough to evangelize the whole world. Don't lose any sleep trying to figure it out. I know it sounds impossible for you to get the large sum of money it will take just to pay off your bills.

Knowing Where Is Not Important

Having exact knowledge **where** the finances you need will come from is not important. What is important is to know **Who** will cause them to be given into your hand. God is the one who will bring them forth. It will be by His miracle power that you receive them.

In His Word, God tells us where we will get these riches. He says there are massive amounts of wealth in this world, and He is about to transfer them to His children.

The Sinners' Wealth

This wealth will come from none other than **the sinners** of this world. That's right! The Bible clearly states that periodically, God takes the money that the **sinful rich** have been stacking up and gives it to His children.

> **"A good man leaveth an inheritance to his children's children: and** *the wealth of the sinner is laid up for the just."*
>
> **Proverbs 13:22**

> **"He that by usury and unjust gain increaseth his substance,** *he shall gather it for him that will pity the poor."*
> **Proverbs 28:8**

God Wants Money In Your Hands

Don't let these verses of Scripture surprise you. Verses like them appear throughout the Word of God. God wants money in your hands so you can get out of debt. He wants you to stop being the servant of the lenders. He actually wants you to be so prosperous that you can **be the lender.**

> **"...and** *thou shalt lend* **unto many nations, and** *thou shalt not borrow."*
> **Deuteronomy 28:12**

Remember, God wants you to **be blessed.** He wants you **out of debt.** He wants you to have enough finances to **be a blessing.** He wants you to be able to reach out to the poor and meet their needs. He also wants you to reach out to the lost with the good news about Jesus that they so desperately need.

The Wicked Ignorantly Gather Wealth

Every moment of every day the wicked gather wealth. They do not even know why they have such an **insatiable appetite** for money. The Lord tells us that they gather this wealth for a people who will bless the poor.

> "... he shall gather it for him that will pity the poor."
> **Proverbs 28:8**

Throughout the world, the wicked wealthy are heaping up riches so they can turn them over to those who are good before God. The good before God are those who have been washed in the blood of Jesus and made righteous by His substitutionary atonement.

> "Though he [the wicked] *heap up silver as the dust,*
> and prepare raiment as the clay;
> He may prepare it, but the just shall put it on, and
> the *innocent shall divide the silver.*"
> **Job 27:16, 17**

Hear the Word of God. We will wear the splendid garments of the wicked, and we will divide their great hoards of silver among ourselves.

Now, I can hear the skeptics saying, "Brother John, I believe what the Bible says, but I have never heard of the great resources of the wicked being given to the children of God."

It Happened to Abraham

Abraham received the gift of great riches from the Egyptians. Make no mistake about it. Abraham's wealth was **not earned.** He was broke before he went down to Egypt. He had no possessions to speak of. Why, he didn't even have a bodyguard!

Not having proper protection caused him to tell everyone that his wife, Sarai, was his sister. He did this to keep the men of Egypt from killing him and taking her.

During this visit, the Pharaoh fell in love with Sarai and declared that she would soon be his wife. Because of his attraction to her, the king made Abraham rich.

> "And he entreated Abram well *for her sake:* and he had sheep, and oxen, and he asses, and menservants, and maidservants, and she asses, and camels."
> **Genesis 12:16**

Eventually, Abraham was forced to admit that Sarai was more than his half-sister. She was, in fact, his wife.

Now, witness the miracle transfer of wealth that took place between the unrighteous Pharaoh and the righteous man of God, Abraham. When the Pharaoh found out that Sarai was married, instead of killing Abraham, he did a very strange thing. He gave Abraham huge amounts of gold, silver, and cattle.

No doubt Pharaoh wanted to curse Abraham, **but all God would allow him to do was to bless him**. He blessed Abraham so much that a very significant statement is made in Scripture about his gifts.

> **"And Abram was** *very rich* **in cattle, in silver, and in gold."**
> **Genesis 13:2**

Notice, not only does the Scripture say Abraham was made rich, but it says he was made **very rich**. Keep in mind that this wealth came from **the most unsuspecting place**. Even though Abraham had lied to the king and made a fool of him, Pharaoh made him rich.

When God decides it is time for the wealth to be transferred to His chosen people, the wicked are unable to stop their urge to bless them.

It Happened to Isaac

While Isaac was living in his homeland, he came upon hard times because of a harsh famine. To add to this pressure, the Philistines had also stopped up his wells. His first thought was to go to Egypt as his father before him had done. However, God told him to stay out of that land. Instead he instructed him to dwell in the country of the Philistines. The famine was raging. Everywhere the land was barren and non-productive. But God made a promise to Isaac that if he would faithfully sow, He would **be faithful** to give him a **hundredfold harvest**.

> "Sojourn in this land, and I will be *with thee,* and will *bless thee;* for unto thee, and unto thy seed, I will give all these countries, and *I will perform the oath which I sware unto Abraham thy father.*"
> **Genesis 26:3**

What had God promised Abraham? He promised that his seed would prosper. Please remember that **you also are the seed of Abraham.** Your God says to you, just as He said to Isaac, **"I will perform the oath which I sware unto Abraham thy father."**

Isaac obeyed, and look what happened.

> "Then Isaac sowed in that land, and received in the same year *an hundredfold:* and the Lord blessed him."
> **Genesis 26:12**

With the money from his hundredfold harvest, Isaac did business among the Philistines until he was rich beyond measure. In a matter of time, that wicked nation's wealth was transferred to him.

> "For he had possession of *flocks,* and possession of *herds,* and great store of *servants*: and *the Philistines envied him.*"
> **Genesis 26:14**

It Happened to Jacob

The most adverse conditions may prevail on your job. It may seem as if you have little chance of advancement, much less a chance of ever really prospering.

But do not overestimate your boss's power to hold back when God says it is **time to release your blessing.** God can move the heart of even the tightest boss. Remember Jacob's boss, Laban? Was there ever a tighter boss than he?

Jacob was cheated by Laban again and again. Why, it looked as if he would never prosper. But as time went by, his faithfulness to God began to turn the tables on wicked Laban. Every time Laban tried to cheat him, **God made a way** for righteous Jacob to prosper from Laban's wealth. In the end, he was made rich with the wealth his wicked boss had tried in vain to withhold from him.

Remember that even if your **boss has plans to hold you down, your God has plans to lift you up!** You cannot be held back by man, for greater is He that is in you than he who is trying to hold you down.

It Happened to the Nation of Israel

Let me share one more example. I remind you of the nation of Israel when they were in Egyptian captivity. After four hundred years in bondage, God released them from their captors.

> "And the Lord said unto Moses, yet will I bring one plague more upon Pharaoh, and upon Egypt; afterwards he will let you go hence: when he shall let you go, he shall surely thrust you out hence altogether.
>
> Speak now in the ears of the people, and let every man *borrow* of his neighbor, and every woman of her neighbor, *jewels of silver, and jewels of gold.*
>
> And the Lord gave the people favor in the sight of the Egyptians . . . ."
>
> **Exodus 11:1-3**

Remember that while the Jews did borrow their wealth, **they never had to pay a penny of it back!** As the Red Sea closed on the Egyptians, **the wealth of the wicked was transferred to the righteous!**

It Is About to Happen to You

Child of God, as we all know, **these are the last days.** According to Scripture, it is once again time for the wealth of the wicked to be transferred into the hands of God's children. Hear the Word of God on this point.

> "Go to now, ye rich men, weep and howl for your miseries that shall come upon you.
>
> Your riches are corrupted, and your garments are motheaten.
>
> Your gold and silver is cankered; and the rust of them shall be a witness against you, and shall eat your flesh as it were fire. *Ye have heaped treasure together for the last days.*"
>
> **James 5:1-3**

The wicked are stacking up their money for **the very day in which we live.** They cannot help it, for they are being **compelled** by God to do so.

> "... to the sinner he giveth travail, to gather and to heap up, that he may give to him that is good before God...."
> **Ecclesiastes 2:26**

Never before in the history of the world have there been such huge pockets of wealth in the earth. It is God's plan to take this wealth and give it to His Church. It will be given to those who will properly use it to fund every righteous work God has planned for these last days.

Get Ready for Your Release

Get ready! God is about to release great sums of wealth into your hands. How do you get your share released to you? **By giving!**

> "Give, and it shall be given unto you; good measure, pressed down, and shaken together, and running over, shall *men* give into your bosom. For with the same measure that ye mete withal it shall be measured to you again."
> **Luke 6:38**

Hear carefully what this verse just said to you. Men — lost men — will give into your bosom with the same measure that you have given into the Gospel.

Ready or not, the great end-time wealth transfer awaits the obedient children of God. He wants you out of debt so you can be a blessing!

I Hope To Hear from You

I hope to hear that the power of debt has been broken, and the miracle of canceled debt has taken place **in your life!** Please share this revelation with others who are under the influence of the spirit of debt. It is my prayer that they also will be released from its grip.

The End

Footnote: If you would like to study more about the transfer of the world's wealth to the children of God, please see John Avanzini's book, <u>The Wealth of the World</u>, published by Harrison House, Tulsa, Oklahoma.

John Avanzini was born in Paramaribo, Surinam, South America, in 1936. He was raised and educated in Texas, and received his doctorate in philosophy from Baptist Christian University, Shreveport, Louisiana. Dr. Avanzini now resides with his wife, Patricia, in Fort Worth, Texas, where he is the Director of His Image Ministries.

Dr. Avanzini's television program, *Principles of Biblical Economics,* is aired five times per day, seven days per week, by more than 550 television stations from coast to coast. He speaks nationally and internationally in conferences and seminars every week. His tape and book ministry is worldwide, and many of his vibrant teachings are now available in tape and book form.

Dr. Avanzini is an extraordinary teacher of the Word of God, bringing forth many of the present truths that God is using in these days to prepare the Body of Christ for His triumphant return.

To contact John Avanzini, write:

John Avanzini
P. O. Box 1057
Hurst, Texas 76053

*Please include your prayer requests and
comments when you write.*

WEALTH TRANSFER SYSTEM

$29.95

This Album contains an outstanding book entitled <u>The</u> <u>Wealth</u> <u>of</u> <u>The</u> <u>World</u> which deals with the transfer of wealth from the world into the Kingdom of GOD!

This Album also includes an edited form of the book (with supporting Scriptures) being read to you so you can get these valuable truths into your spirit even while you drive or work!

FOUNDATION PACK

$29.95

The Foundation Pack contains <u>Powerful Principles of Increase</u>, a series of 90 lessons on the principles of biblical prosperity.

This album includes three tapes containing 377 Scriptures on giving, receiving, and God's abundance that will give you a true picture of how God feels about money. This information will help you break the traditions that have kept you from receiving from God!

THE SCHOOL OF BIBLICAL ECONOMICS

Home Edition

$140.00 Worth of Tapes and Books for only $70.00

$70.00

INCLUDED:

* **GOD'S WEALTH TRANSFER SYSTEM**
    - 1 book - <u>The Wealth of the World</u>
      God's proven wealth transfer system.
    - 3 tapes - An edited version of this book with supporting Scriptures.

* **BUILDING THE FOUNDATIONS OF BIBLICAL ECONOMICS**
    - 1 book - <u>Powerful Principles of Increase</u>
      Ninety powerful lessons on biblical economics.
    - 3 tapes - 377 Scriptures dealing with giving, receiving, and God's abundance.

* **THE SCHOOL OF BIBLICAL ECONOMICS TAPES**
    - 8 tapes - The teachings of John and Patricia Avanzini from an actual School of Biblical Economics.

* **STUDY GUIDE**
    This study guide highlights the books and tapes in this home course to help you better understand God's principles of biblical economics, and how you can put them to work in your life.

Order form, see Page 190

Based on principles he has seen proven in his own life, Dr. Avanzini provides you with the laws of harvest, God's plan for you to live abundantly!

$8.00

30 60 HUNDREDFOLD

You will learn:

How to determine whether you are planting in good or bad soil.

The importance of replanting part of your harvest.

How to maintain the "crops" until harvest.

The importance of giving and the benefits God has for faithful givers.

How to apply the laws of harvest and use the principles God has established.

FAITH EXTENDERS

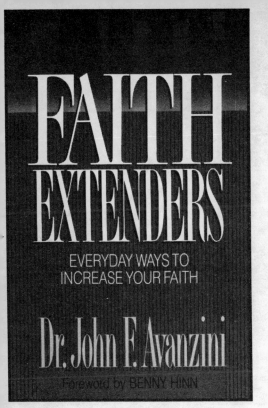

$8.00

**GOD IS REACHING
OUT TO YOU.
IS YOUR FAITH
REACHING BACK
TO HIM?**

Sometimes we are so overwhelmed by our needs and problems that we think even God's power is not big enough to help us. Our faith is often too small to reach out to Him and receive His grace.

In Faith Extenders, John Avanzini distills from the Bible the secrets of how to act in ways that make our faith grow stronger. The men and women we recognize as Bible heroes were human beings just like us. They suffered, they had problems, they failed, and they sinned. Then what made them heroes? It was their ability to focus on situations, events, people and simple things as ways of magnifying their faith. Faith Extenders teaches us how to respond to our daily circumstances in a manner that increases our faith and helps us to tap into the power God wants us to have.

STOLEN PROPERTY RETURNED

$6.00

When You Have Been "Ripped Off," "Robbed" and "Stolen From," Where Can You Go for Help?

There Is an Answer in the Bible That Always Gets Results!

Every one of us has had something of value stolen from him. It may have been in business, a family relationship, a wayward child, a promotion on the job, or even large sums of money. In the midst of these terrible assaults we seem powerless to recover our losses.

John Avanzini reveals to us, in Stolen Property Returned, how to take the thief into the heavenly courtroom, where God is the judge and Jesus is the prosecuting attorney. In this courtroom the verdict is guaranteed in our favor.

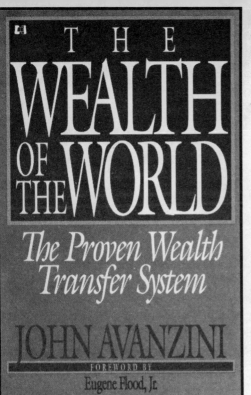

$7.00

THE WEALTH OF THE WORLD

The Wealth of the World answers the following questions and others with balanced, biblical teaching that will change your thinking about money and will open the doors for you to walk in overflowing abundance.

Is it true? Does the wealth of the sinner really belong to the just, the righteous of God?

Is it really God's desire to see all of His children blessed?

What purpose would God have in blessing His children to such an extent?

ALWAYS ABOUNDING

THE WAY TO PROSPER IN GOOD TIMES, BAD TIMES, ANY TIME

John Avanzini

$6.00

ALWAYS ABOUNDING

DYNAMIC! POWERFUL! LIFE-CHANGING!

Always Abounding is truth that will bring you into a new dimension of abundant living. **_It is an investment plan from God's Word that cannot fail._**

If you are someone who desires:
- promotion on your job
- prosperity in your business
- abundance in recession
- security in your job and your finances
- more than enough to give

Then _Always Abounding_ is for you!

No matter what the current economic circumstances indicate, no matter what the state of the country looks like, you can have more than enough.
You have God's Word on it!

This book could be the beginning of a whole new day for you with the glorious supply that God has in store for those who give cheerfully unto Him.

POWERFUL PRINCIPLES *of* INCREASE

Are you tired of being continuously short of the finances you need to fully and completely obey God?

Would you like to begin to operate in a bold new cycle of abundance with God?

Do you want to have a part in financing the great end-time harvest?

$9.00

Powerful Principles of Increase is a series of lessons designed to help you experience the financial breakthrough you have been desiring. Some of the lessons include:
- How You Can Reap in a Recession
- 10 Truths About Money
- Five Major Mistakes About Money
- The Abundance of God
- God—The Greatest Giver
- Five Kinds of Giving

Learn how you can experience God's abundance and be a blessing to others.

In this exciting book by John Avanzini, we have key after key spelled out from the Word of God showing us we can take the resources of this world and use them to establish God's Kingdom! Let's read them and then do them in Jesus' name!
PAUL F. CROUCH
Trinity Broadcasting Network, Inc.

ORDER FORM

NAME _____

ADDRESS _____

CITY _____ STATE _____ ZIP _____ PHONE _____

☐VISA   ☐MASTERCARD   ☐CHECK

CREDIT CARD # _____ EXP. DATE _____

DESCRIPTION	UNIT COUNT	UNIT PRICE	AMOUNT
30/60/Hundredfold		$8.00	
Always Abounding		$6.00	
Faith Extenders		$8.00	
Powerful Principles of Increase		$9.00	
Stolen Property Returned		$6.00	
Wealth of the World		$7.00	
The School of Biblical Economics		$70.00	
Wealth Transfer System		$29.95	
Foundation Pack		$29.95	
		TOTAL AMOUNT	

☐Check here for 1 year's FREE subscription to Dr. John Avanzini's "BIBLICAL ECONOMICS UPDATE"

These books can be purchased from your local bookstores, or by writing:

HIS PUBLISHING CO.
P.O. Box 1096
Hurst, Texas 76053
(817) 485-5997
For orders, call: 1-800-962-8337